YOUR FIELD GUIDE TO
Community Building

Vicki Luther & Mary Emery

Heartland Center for Leadership Development

Heartland Center for Leadership Development
941 "O" Street, Suite 920
Lincoln, NE 68508
Phone: (402) 474-7667 Fax: (402) 474-7672
Toll Free: (800) 927-1115
www.heartlandcenter.info

Book Design: Reynold Peterson

Printed in the United States of America

ISBN 0-9747027-0-6

This is for Nette Nelson,
who built community with passion and practice
and who lives in our hearts forever.

Preface

The Heartland center has, since its creation, paid attention to the needs of small towns and neighborhoods. Our mission is to develop local leadership that responds to the challenges of the future. With that in mind, this new resource was developed for community builders of all types and persuasions.

Because of the support of the W.K. Kellogg Foundation, we were able to gather stories, experiences and suggested tools and techniques. *Your Field Guide to Community Building* was created from not only our own experiences, but that of our colleagues and associates. All together this amounts to nearly 1000 years of working in communities!

We've added a compact disk to this publication that includes full transcripts of interviews, video selections and a key word search capability so that readers can supplement this text with real stories from real communities. We're eager for feedback and hope that you'll contact us with your own stories about community building.

Milan Wall & Vicki Luther
Co-Directors
Heartland Center

Acknowledgements

The following community builders contributed to this publication and project, along with the staff of the Center for Rural Strategies. The support of the W.K. Kellogg Foundation and Caroline Carpenter is also gratefully acknowledged.

Mickey Beach, Oregon
Dorothy Bennet, Tennessee
Jim Birdsall, Idaho
Mark Blucher, Vermont
Hubert Brandon, Alabama
James Calvin, Maryland
Edyael Casaperalta, Texas
Jean Ann Casey, Oklahoma
Ernesto Castillo, Nebraska
Anita Chacon, Colorado
Helen Cline, Oklahoma
Rick Eberhard, Kansas
Ruth Gerber, Nebraska
Gordon Goodwin, Texas
Mema-shua Regina Grant, Nebraska
Diane Green, Idaho
Francisco Guarjardo, Texas
Rita Henroid, Missouri

Peter Hille, Kentucky
Carl Hughes, Alabama
Ron Hustedde, Kentucky
Ellen Lierk, Nebraska
Felix Lopez, Colorado
Joseph Luther, Nebraska
Lew McCreary, West Virginia
Megan O'Byrne, Nebraska
Midge Palmer, Ohio
Mark Peterson, Arkansas
Reshell Ray, Nebraska
Randy Ross, Minnesota
Olga Sanchez, Nebraska
Leon Sharpe, Missouri
Barry Shioshita, Colorado
Lillian Winnenberg, Ohio
Angie Woodward, Kentucky

Contents

Introduction

Have you ever returned from a workshop or conference filled with enthusiasm to try out a new group process technique? Have you ever found yourself driving to a meeting trying to remember that technique and wondering if you should really try it out? And what about the nagging question of whether or not your presence is, in fact, making any difference? Anyone who works in rural areas and small towns knows that feeling of working alone, wondering about progress and trying to explain to family and friends what exactly it is that you do for a living!

This publication is intended as a Field Guide for community builders. It was developed to provide a helpful source for both motivation and improved technique. And it was developed with the help of community builders like you.

In November 2001, 40 community builders and activists joined together in a retreat in Lincoln, Nebraska. Facilitated by the staff of the Heartland Center for Leadership Development and supported by funding from the W. K. Kellogg

Foundation, this retreat offered a chance for reflection on the passion and practice of community building. What keeps us going? What have we learned about what really works?

Each participant was asked to complete a journal and a videotaped interview. Both the journal and the videotaping followed a general outline of the community building process and were intended to capture stories of success, challenges, inspiration and innovation in working with groups of citizens toward community improvement.

This is the core of the definition of community building that serves as the basis for this field guide.

Why community *building*? The traditional terms of community organizing and community development have, over time, evolved into complex terms with historic and vernacular meanings that blur the important work of creating local capacity. Some community builders use community organizing to refer to an issue-driven collective action that confronts the power structure. The term community development is often confused with federal programs for the improvement of physical infrastructure.

By using the term *community building*, we have chosen a clear emphasis on the effort to increase local capacity. But capacity for what? We mean the capacity of community residents to take collective action towards community improvement. That means that a community builder/activist works to increase the skills of individuals, strengthen reciprocal relationships and make networks within and outside the community open and responsive to needs.

The community builders/ activists that took part in the Heartland Center retreat shared a process that reached across content areas and local topics. That basic process served as the framework for the retreat and this Field Guide. The systematic process included working with a representative group, identifying issues and resources, creating a plan with vision, goals and actions, all the while attending to issues of broad involvement, coaching and evaluation. Much discussion at the retreat made it obvious that the process included forward and backward progress, repeating steps and recycling.

What's Your Role? What Does it Mean?

One consequence of the role of community builder is that the community builder/activist can become invisible. Working behind the scenes, supporting and coaching local leaders, the community builder often lets others take credit for change and innovation. This can, of course, create havoc with accountability in very traditional organizations or with office mates whose hours are nine to five rather than

evening hours with meetings that last until midnight. Somehow the community builder has to explain to co-workers why community building requires flexible hours and a variety of staff support.

Community builders must sometimes make peace with accountability systems that are artificial and don't relate to the work of community building. Counting attendance at a meeting is a prime example. If only a few attend, the meeting can be seen as a failure. However, if those few are residents who have never before been involved and are new and emerging leaders, the impact is considerable.

One implication of the "behind the scenes" role of the community builder is that funding for this work is often difficult to obtain and a struggle to justify. Rewards often go to those whose work is most visible. It takes public relations and marketing skills to make the invisible process tangible to county commissioners, foundations and other stakeholders.

A capacity building approach is process-focused rather than product-focused. Capacity building does, of course, include products, but, as we all know, it's harder to sell process than product. And this makes the

role of the community builder more difficult. The argument of process versus product is still alive and well, even though common sense would tell us that you have to balance both in order to succeed.

All of theses aspects of the community builder/activist role also have implications for the ethics of the work of community building and how we handle our own needs for recognition, appreciation and ownership of projects. It's a delicate balance between our own needs and the ethics that demand involvement that builds the capacity of local leaders to do without our help.

A Field Guide for You

Community building is NOT rocket science. Rocket science is easier. While complex, rocket science deals with unchanging, predictable laws such as gravity. There are many variables in rocket science, but the issues are basically engineering problems. Community building deals with very complex and constantly changing issues, such as power structures, politics, territory and history. And that's at the community level! Factor in the varieties of human behavior and personality, and you can see that community building demands a wide scope of skills and determination.

The skills and experience base are important. It's vital to know several ways to help a group make a decision, for example, so that you can respond to the group's needs for structure. It's vital to be able to adapt a technique to match an on-the-spot development in a project. And, perhaps most of all, it's vital to know how to take care of yourself as you work with a community.

This Field Guide is intended to serve as a support to the community builder by providing the stories of other community builders as they make their way through the process and how they troubleshoot as problems arise. Perhaps most importantly, it is how to keep the passion alive that makes the practice of community building so important.

From the Field

The old admonition in community building is to "watch out for the bear in the woods. When you least expect it, this bear will jump out from behind a tree and kill you or your project. In this case, it was almost all three—including the bear, of course.

It had been a letter-perfect participatory process. All the classic activies had been used: all the empowerment had occurred; all the clients were in charge and I was in the best position. I was in the back of the Grange Hall eating cookies.

This had been a yearlong effort at self-determination in which the residents of a rural area had developed their own specific plan. I served as the coach, educator, catalyst and change agent—all that

stuff. We'd completed SWOT analysis, nominal group process, brainstorming, needs assessments and filled sheets of newsprint in small group work. They had done their own environmental analysis using the overlay mapping of Ian McHarg. The project had gone so well that I was planning to write a case study of how it should be done!

The local folks had planned the meeting with my help. I waited in the kitchen while they reviewed the agenda, announced the starting and ending times, and reviewed the desired outcomes of the meeting. Various task forces and work groups were introduced and started to explain their work. I was SO proud of them as they took charge of their future and demonstrated such capacity and self-help results.

At this moment, that bear jumped out from behind a tree. A local landowner who had been in Europe for the year rose to his feet to voice his objections. He stood up and in a very loud voice announced, "Never in my life time will this plan come to pass." He continued, "Only over my dead body. At this moment, he fell over dead."

General chaos ensued. Many steel folding chairs were knocked over and scattered. Members of the audience included physicians, nurses and volunteer firefighters. The rest of us backed away as the professionals took over and began CPR. The firefighter was on call, radioed his unit and soon sirens could be heard as the fire truck raced to the Grange Hall. In a short time, there were two fire trucks, an ambulance and a lot of people in the parking lot. All the nearby residents thought the Grange Hall was on fire and came running to help.

After everyone and all the emergency vehicles had departed, I walked back into the Grange Hall and looked at the jumble. The environmental maps were slowly coming untaped from the walls and half-hung there like decorations from yesterday's party. The chairs had been returned to their stacks, the coffee and cookies were gone. I rolled up my maps, charts and all those really good plans. When my wife arrived at 9 p.m. (the time of the anticipated magnificent finish), I was sitting despondent on the steps, deep in misery.

The bear had, indeed, come out of the woods. The happy ending here was that the shouter's life had been saved by his fellow residents, and in his gratitude, he actually helped finance the project!

Always anticipate the bear in the woods. What will **you** do when the bear jumps out at you?

—*Joe Luther*
Nebraska

Chapter One
First Steps

The Same But Different

One of the most fascinating aspects of community building is the discovery that all communities are the same but different. Context changes while many issues are constant. Small towns all over our country are dealing with issues of affordable housing, health care, teen pregnancy, senior citizen care, poverty, jobs—the list goes on and on. What changes are the ways that communities deal with the issues.

Certainly no community group enjoys the message that their town is just like the one down the road or in the neighboring state. On the other hand, similarities can also be motivating. Many community builders use case studies that compare communities to demonstrate a shared concern (You're not the only ones with this problem) or to offer examples of problem-solving responses (Take a look at how this town dealt with this issue). In either case, community building has to use

that ambiguity of same but different to its advantage.

What does seem to be standard among communities is the need to recruit new volunteers and create or expand existing groups. Community service and volunteerism have become greater struggles for community residents as the economy demands two incomes and family schedules become more crowded. Forming a group as a first step in a community building process isn't merely a matter of naming a few elected officials and then relying on the Rotarians to fill the gap!

The community builder often begins with an existing, core group that has identified a need or at least asked for help in some way. Expanding a group can be even trickier than forming a representative group. In both cases, however, the need for true community representation should take the forefront as a genuine concern and motivating issue for invitations.

Why Bother?

A core group is a touchstone for the community builder. Aside from the obvious (you have to start with someone!), a core group that truly reflects the mix of the community will provide some insurance against decisions that merely repeat history or preserve the status quo. The more reflective of the community the group is, the more likely it is that the group's behavior and decisions will, in fact, fit the community context. That doesn't mean those decisions and behaviors will necessarily be comfortable or even wise.

However, the community builder has to match representation with accountability so that the decisions and behaviors are really part of the community as a whole.

If you work only with the same contacts for every community project, your perspective may begin to match theirs. This narrowing of perspective may come into play when working with community builders trained in specific backgrounds such as health care, K-12 education or natural resource conservation, for example, who tend to work in their own areas, and who may not see community connections across issues. A community group that represents various age, social, economic, cultural and occupational backgrounds will widen the conversation about an issue to allow for validation and innovation. In this way, that representative community group can save the community builder from viewing a project too narrowly.

There's also an ethical dimension to the representative group notion. A time-honored community building adage says, "People who are affected by a decision have a right to influence that decision." This was true for the English colonists and it's also true for every parent-teachers group, youth center board or planning commission. As community builders, part of the capacity building role is to increase the skills people need to make their voices heard and be involved in decisions that affect them. The goal is to help every voice be heard in a safe and supportive environment.

When community residents become part of a core group, whether it's called a steering committee or something else, it's possible to transfer skills that become not only part of the individual's life but also part of the community. Building capacity in this way makes forming a representative group that includes first time volunteers or emerging leaders important to the overall impact of community building.

Do Your Homework

It seems like common sense to try to learn as much as possible about a community before you begin working with a group there. However, there are situations where either there's no time or we think we already know everything! Web pages are becoming more common, and basic economic and demographic information is readily available from state and federal agencies.

It's also helpful to talk to other service providers that might be working in the community. Public school consultants and public health nurses, for example, offer good perspectives on local history and the players in town. The suggestion here is to explore other sources in addition to the usual conversations with the mayor, economic development director or planning director.

Information gathering really never stops since a community builder has to keep eyes and ears open for community feedback. That's not to say that you should take an approach that only collects data. Data can be seductive since you can collect it forever and postpone taking any action (or risk) that way. However, you should be able to make conversation about local issues, economy or history.

Doing your homework also helps you to see potential problems with individuals, organizations and politics. Being able to anticipate where controversy might develop will also help to identify recruits for a truly representative group.

How Were You Invited?

It can make a huge difference to your reception in a community if you've been invited rather than just arrived because a town is on your list to visit or part of your agency's plan of work. And, of course, who extended the invitation can also either open all the doors to the movers and shakers or slam shut some faction within the community. It's smart to get to an understanding of the local reputation of the folks who invited you because that will influence the way others react to you. It's a question of credibility.

Getting clear on your invitation also includes clarifying the expectations the group has of you and the work you'll do with the community. If everyone you talk to has a different view of your role, you may need to design a work session just to clarify what you'll do and what the group should expect. It may seem a luxury to formalize expectations in a letter of agreement but many community builders typically do just that. This is especially true if financial arrangements are part of the exceptions, either for fees or even for travel expenses.

The Big Issues

We have all experienced what it's like to be on the outside of a group. Expand that to the larger community and you can extrapolate the bigger issues of power, racism, economic stratification and gender bias. The greatest challenge to forming a representative group is facing these issues in a way that will be useful to everyone involved. The word "useful" is very important and has to be seen from several perspec-tives, including short-term and long-term impacts. A confrontation might work unless it results in a worse situation in the long run.

Established leaders may not be comfortable with admitting that they prefer not to include an outsider because of language, race, poverty, age or gender. But the exclusion will, in fact, be acted out in the way an invitation is sent and to whom, or perhaps in questioning the capability of someone to participate. An example would be a leader saying, "It's not fair to ask those people to be on the project since they'd just be overwhelmed, out of their depth."

Exclusion must be addressed and it's up to the community builder to find a way that opens the door to true representation. Sometimes this may involve questioning strategies, specific suggestions or persistent reminders. Occasionally, some degree of confrontation may be required.

Another issue is the need for renewing representation in the group. In any community project, life does, in fact, get in the way of volunteers' time commitments, and every group will need to pay attention to keeping the group representative.

Paying Attention to Strategies and Techniques

1. Community Analysis

A basic strategy is based on helping the group to analyze the community and therefore identifying the participants that should be recruited. This can be done with a simple brainstorming session (What are the groups that make up our community?), then following the listing with a nomination of individuals that might represent a group for recruitment. A simple matrix of skills and interests needed for the project is another approach. Many community builders use storytelling about the community and individuals to begin the analysis process. More elaborate techniques might include the use of demographic data from state or federal sources, survey work or focus groups.

Power analysis might also be necessary for forming a representative group. Identifying stakeholders, champions and sponsors can be very helpful. The identification of opponents and critics might add a useful dimension to a representative group. Sometimes having the naysayer at the table can serve to keep criticism in balance.

2. Expanding Personal Networks

"Each one bring one" is a tried and true method for increasing involvement and can be used to broaden the membership of a beginning, core group. In this case, it's helpful to create an activity or discussion that allows the core group to reflect on personal networks. While core group members might see obvious connections, a bit of exploration will help them identify other networks that might not be so obvious. For example, having kids in the same youth group with the bank president's family might present a network to recruit participation from that institution.

3. Look Beyond First Impacts

If a project targets a specific audience, those are the folks that are usually brought into a working group to advise and plan. However, looking beyond the first impact clients might prove fruitful in identifying new members. Getting single moms back in the labor force has impacts on the extended family, so grandparents might be recruited.

Affordable housing projects do well to involve developers and bankers. Leadership training can change the dynamics in families, so local pastors or church representatives might be recruited.

4. Always Look for the Kids

The presence of youth in any community group seems to improve the behavior of adults. It's awkward for adults to exhibit pettiness or mean-spirited competition when the group includes youngsters. It's true that participation is easier on the kids if you invite more than one to attend meetings so that there's some comfort in numbers. Youth representatives can be drawn from the academic elite or be all-around volunteers already involved in many youth organizations. Another approach is to ask teachers to identify capable but uninvolved students and invite several to participate. In any case, there's no rationale for excluding the youth from any community project no matter what the topic might be.

Many adult-only groups will insist that they've tried to get youth involved but had only negative experiences. This usually means that they invited a student government representative and then ignored her during their meeting or had nervous teens present but separated from the group by sitting in the back and giggling throughout the meeting. Youth involvement works only if it's taken seriously before, during and after the meeting. Kids need a coaching session before the meeting. This can take the form of asking them in advance to prepare to introduce themselves and say a few words about a club they belong to or even what they like best about the community. During the meeting or work session, it's also very important to ask the youth for opinions or questions so that their voices are heard several times. And, after the meeting, giving an information-gathering assignment, especially Internet research, will extend their involvement into the next meeting.

5. Pay Attention to the Details

The location, the meeting room itself, seating arrangements or an informal assumption about how to dress for a meeting can all send a signal of inclusion or exclusion. Make sure that the meeting location and site are truly neutral or positive. Don't be too casual or haphazard about seating arrangements with a new group. Instead use table tents, nametags, table discussions or fun introductions to get everyone started on an equal basis. Don't let participants hide behind important sounding titles.

6. Search out Surprising Partnerships

While at first it seems obvious who the stakeholders should be for a community project, there's always room for new and surprising partnerships among organizations. Look for groups that don't normally work together. Involving the arts community in economic development or the historical society in planning for the future are good examples. Rural and urban connections are also surprising and well worth the effort of reaching out and connecting. Local organizations are often chapters of national groups that can offer support through training materials, or Internet connections.

Troubleshooting

Here are some typical problems encountered by community builders in the first steps of forming a representative group focusing on a community project.

Problems with the Powers That Be

If you're getting resistance from those that fund or control the project and the message is clear that true representation is not a top priority, you have several options:

- Be sure you're interpreting the situation correctly.
- Find a champion whose credibility will support you and start visiting and persuading.
- Create a triangle of concern with two other co-sponsoring organizations that will push the representation issue, again removing the spotlight from you.
- Make the issue of representation public through conversation on the record at meetings or with the help of the media.

Problems with Dropouts

You had an invitation list of a really representative group, but after one meeting, only a few folks are showing up. If keeping the group together is one of your problems, you have several options:

- Check to make sure you've invited the right person. For example, invite someone from the Senior Center, but not necessarily the director who might not have time.
- Find the right person—ask the invitees to find a replacement (a personal appeal).
- Try making the meetings more informal, fun or interesting with food and maybe some type of information exchange (offer some benefits for participation).
- Try a buddy system of matched pairs in the group to remind folks of the meeting times.
- Take a look at how the purpose of the group or project is written and make sure it's clear and sounds important and useful.
- In all cases, make every effort to get the group to help with recruitment and commitment issues.

Problems with Hidden Agendas or At Odds Purpose

In a perfect world, the community builder would sense that members of the group have an agenda that they want to impose on others. Stacking the representative group with folks that agree with that agenda can be a problem. However, as the group forms, these agendas might not be clear or members might bring with them a purpose that is at odds with the community project. Here are some options:

- Spend some start-up time making sure everyone understands the purpose of the group and the project.
- Find a way to remind the group of its purpose such as beginning each meeting with the local vision statement or description of the project.
- Get lots of information, especially local history, to anticipate group members with well-known grudges or personal agendas.
- Don't assume that because people are willing to be inclusive that they will also share power.
- Be prepared to involve the group in decision making about the purpose and/or community project. This involvement should be as public and as inclusive as possible.
- Spend time with everyone in the group, not just special

friends. In this way, you can stay alert and key in to any gossip or politics.

Problems with a Group that Keeps Changing

Keeping the group representative might mean adding or changing members in the course of a community project. If you have problems on how to mesh the newcomers with the old-timers, here are some suggestions:

- Regularly hold an orientation discussion for newcomers, usually 30 minutes before a meeting or work session.
- Develop a simple Fact Sheet about the project that can be used to help newcomers. Remember to use large type and translate if necessary.
- Match up newcomers with old-timers who can give them the background information personally.
- Use some type of introduction activity at every meeting. Even if everyone is acquainted, let each learn something new about one another.
- Give newcomers a special color nametag or cup so that everyone else knows to talk to them at the break.

From the Field

The Scenario

In Alliance, Nebraska, the challenge is getting people involved in community development in the absence of crisis. Alliance is a vital community, yet long-range trends do not bode well for it: it is not the largest trade center in the region; it is located 90 miles off the Interstate; and it is losing its young adults following college graduation. At the same time, Alliance has thriving businesses, good city government, access to education, and an expanding hospital. The development effort identified a specific need to create a fund to attract businesses with good jobs to its community. Creating such a fund with no crisis looming is challenging.

Tools and Techniques Used to Respond to the Issue

Alliance's challenge is getting people involved in community development. Those working on the City's community development effort were able to implement or employ numerous techniques to respond to this need.

- A weekly radio program during which statistics and concerns were discussed.
- Board training involving the need to influence change.

- An annual report and program reviewing the economy.
- Regularly relating stories about communities and their experiences with incentive funds.
- Selection of key members of the community to serve on the economic development board so that the story of the need for a fund is widespread.
- Presentation of programs to service groups.
- Use of media, including the Internet, to get citizens' attention.
- Bringing in experts from out of town.

Lessons Learned from the Experience

- The most valuable contribution citizens can give to development is their attention. We are all so busy that finding ways to get the message heard can be challenging.
- There is a need to take a concept from the very general to the specific and tell people directly how this issue affects them. Finding a way to tell of the need and touch the heart is helpful.

- Some people will not support economic development because they like the community the way it is and do not consider that the city is changing. Economic development is the business of directing those changes to the positive.
- Look for partners who understand the need for development.
- Building a positive attitude in the community will result in more action. When faced with challenge, a positive attitude will see the community out of a negative situation. Every rural community faces tough challenges like losing a doctor, a grocery store, or a government office. The key is not getting discouraged and creating a group of positive citizens who are willing to respond.

—Ellen Lierk
Nebraska

Chapter Two
Developing Group Capacity

We live our lives in groups, whether it's our family of origin or the one we construct, the classes we start in pre-school days or the clubs we join as adults. Every group is different and changes to some degree with the addition of a new member. The fascinating dimension of groups within communities is that there are some patterns of behavior that make it easier to lead, facilitate and participate. One of these patterns of behavior has to do with the simple division of the group task and the group maintenance. Every group does have a task, even if the task is recreational. Every group has to maintain relationships within the group itself in order to sustain itself. If a group only works together, then no social needs will be met. If only socializing occurs and nothing is ever accomplished, the members will be dissatisfied. The balance between these two—task and maintenance—reflects the health and the capacity of the group to continue.

The manner in which the community builder interacts with the group can either help the group to become healthy and sustain itself or be dependent on the outsider for direction, support and validation. Which is the more helpful approach for the community builder? Or to ask the question another way, which approach results in more significant impact in the long run? Developing group capacity is clearly the approach that has the most impact on the community.

Why Bother?

Group capacity, then, is really the bottom line for community building. Think of it this way. If a group can get a job done (task) and also continue to work together in a way that satisfies the members (maintenance), then that group can serve as a building block for the community at large. You do have to start somewhere! Starting with a focus on group capacity is a strategy that will have both short- and long-term rewards.

As a community builder's strategy or approach, developing group capacity means blending the transfer of practical skills with facilitating the interaction of the group towards completion of a goal. A goal might be some type of community betterment project. How does this occur? A basic first step is clarifying the task and maintenance issues as they develop in the group. Helping a community group to understand the purpose of the group (why are we gathered here? What are we supposed to do? Is there a charge or direction already set for us?) is the first step. Defining the task also helps to keep the group on track and can serve as a consistent refer-

ence point when distractions and tangents threaten to take the group off in a new direction. Task roles usually revolve around getting the work done. Some common task roles that individuals take on in a group include setting the agenda, proposing actions, asking for decisions and making assignments.

Maintenance involves issues that occur simultaneously with task definition or purpose of the group. Maintenance is certainly just as important as task. The term maintenance is a term for the behaviors within the group that either maintain the relationships or destroy them. This goes beyond politeness, although civility is an important behavior dimension in community groups.

Maintenance can also refer to the various roles that keep the group going. These roles might include: an information seeker who always asks questions, a timekeeper who mentions deadlines, a convener who pulls the group together, or a tension reliever who can make a joke and help everyone to relax. The roles are numerous and vary from group to group, but the community builder has to be able to recognize the players and especially note when an important maintenance function is missing. Some maintenance roles are obvious—someone has to attend to introductions, for example. While others, such as the tension-reliever, can be less noticeable.

Avoiding Dependency

One of the best motivations for developing group capacity is the avoidance of dependency on the part of the community group. If the community builder consistently runs every meeting, takes care of all logistics, handles all the research and proposes all the decisions, what does the group learn how to do? In an ideal world, community builders could actually work behind the scenes, never step up front at a community meeting and simply be the organizing support system for the resident leaders in town.

There are, of course, some problems with that scenario that might lead one to believe we don't really work in an ideal world! One problem is the fear factor among residents. Fear can motivate a variety of reactions to being asked to take on leadership roles in groups.

Some people need a lot of support and will take only very small steps towards a leadership position. They may be willing to help and gradually take on more responsibility. These folks have a fear of public speaking or making mistakes. Others want to control everything and fear losing control. In both cases, the community builder has to finesse the shared roles and provide opportunities for group members to learn and practice skills while balancing the participation so that nobody dominates the group.

Another inherent problem for the community builder who is working on the development of group capacity is the reward and accountability systems already in place. Many community builders work for agencies or organizations that require justification of community work through documentation of meetings attended, grants written or projects completed.

How does a community builder balance the need to document her or his work while still developing group capacity and independence? This can be tricky, of course. One way to deal with this type of accountability is to make sure that group capacity (or independence) is an intended outcome from the beginning. A community builder can document group members learning and practicing skills such as leading a discussion or running a meeting.

Another way to make sure that the development of group capacity fits into the accountability system of the community builder is to collect examples of how group experiences are transferred to other community efforts. For example, if brainstorming and prioritizing items are demonstrated and then used in one meeting, do those techniques ever show up elsewhere in the community? If so, there's real evidence that progress towards group capacity building is underway.

Look at the development of group capacity and contrast coaching versus technical assistance. In a coaching situation, skills training, practice sessions and feedback—all types of support—are offered but the participant, not the coach, performs the task. In this way, a community builder can make sure that learning is transferred and new behaviors are tried and refined. More about coaching is found in Chapter 7.

It's really not effective to listen to someone else talk about the importance of authentic representa-

tion in a community project group. However, planning an activity before the meeting and then offering directions and engaging in group discussion and analysis of the problem of representation can teach a variety of skills. The *experience*, then, offers a chance to try out some new ways of working together and confirms the teaching/learning opportunity. The capacity of the group and the individual is developed.

Leadership through Group Process

Coaching versus technical assistance leaves a residue of skills in the community. This approach offers a way to create leadership through the practice of sound group process design and implementation. Many individuals, while active volunteers, will refuse the title of leader or in some way reject the idea of themselves as leaders. This reluctance can be an obstacle to widening the circle of involvement in a community project.

Group process skills can build confidence among participants who are more comfortable in smaller groups. Participants can take turns acting as a recorder, leading a discussion, or distributing materials. These elements of structured activities can be designed to provide short, manageable practice sessions that gradually build to a more formal role. Once the group is accustomed to brainstorming, using newsprint to record, and working in pairs or trios, then the participants' comfort level will increase.

Group process skills for the community builder are of paramount importance. These skills are commonly seen in the facilitation role that helps a group arrive at a decision.

Communication skills such as paraphrasing questions, behavior descriptions, proposing actions, and clarifying choices are among the standards needed to manage the process of the group. However, design skills are also very important—the ability to create a structure for participants to practice leadership is perhaps the most important way to develop group capacity.

Paying Attention to Strategies and Techniques

1. Structure Not Content

Providing adequate structure for a group can enhance participation, especially if the individuals in the group can fill in the content. An example of this is an activity in which trios or pairs are asked to talk for ten minutes and develop a list of the first five actions required to achieve a group goal. This offers a concrete, specific structure and a time limit but does not dictate content. The question or discussion assignment can vary, of course, but the structure is still helpful.

2. Individual, Then Small Group, Then Large Group Activities

Designing activities in which an individual works first alone, then in a pair or trio, and then finally in the entire, large group can develop individual skills and maximize participation. Offering even a moment or two for an individual to reflect can greatly improve the quality of the discussion.

3. Translate Other Experiences

Many group members have life experiences that can translate into skills applicable to a community project. One way to develop group capacity is to create situations in which, for example, a business owner realizes that his marketing ideas can be applied to letting the community know about a project, or a parent understands that the organizational skills it takes to plan a birthday party can be applied to a town hall meeting. This translation of experience into the here and now

of a project is a foundation element of adult education. Even the simple question, "What do you need to do to go on a family vacation?" can result in a list of all the steps of a strategic plan.

4. Rotate Assignments

Taking turns acting as chairperson for a group is an excellent technique for building group capacity. Other assignments that can be rotated include taking notes or minutes, recording at a flip chart, serving as a timekeeper and leading a discussion at the end of a meeting to build the next agenda or consider what went well and what might be changed.

5. Put the Jigsaw Together

Anytime you can divide information into several parts, you can use a strategy that requires each person to learn only one part, teach that to others and then learn the rest from others. For example, if there are three committee reports, each on a single page handout, you can form a trio and assign one report to each person. Allow some time to read and prepare for the trio, then let each member take a turn and teach or share her report with the other two. This is a much better approach than having an entire group listen to one single voice after another offering a report. This type of information sharing can also work to build confidence and maximize participation.

6. Everything Counts!

No task is too small to receive recognition from the group. Using the approach that everything counts toward group capacity allows all types of contributions and opens the door to experimentation by participants who might be reluctant to take on highly visible leadership positions. Starting small in community participation is a perfectly legitimate way to recruit volunteers and develop individual and group capacity.

Troubleshooting

Following are some typical problems encountered by community builders as the effort is made to build group capacity.

Too Many Trees, No Forest at All

Some groups are so intent on steps and procedures that the larger topics of group health and capacity are ignored. This is often especially true in hierarchical groups with roles that are rigid. Here are some options to consider:

- Try some self-evaluation by group members. This might take the form of a worksheet that lets members rate how the group communicates or makes decisions.
- An informal evaluation at the end of a meeting or work session can take the form of a newsprint sheet with a + (positive), – (negative) and Δ (change) columns that record group member responses.
- Include in an agenda a discussion of best/worst groups that members have known. This sets the stage for a discussion of the group's strengths and weaknesses.
- Lead an activity in which each member completes a work sheet on what she or he would like to learn from being part of the group. Personal learning goals can be shared in pairs.
- Brainstorm with group members what they like best about the group. This is one way to identify gaps in managing task versus maintenance.

Problems with Members that are Too Quiet or Too Dominant

Either extreme of participation can be disruptive to the group and derail the goal of increasing group capacity. Balancing the talkers and the non-talkers will also improve the group process. Here are some options:

- Give the dominant person the role of recorder. This tends to control talkers.
- Use a poll or survey of the group to make sure every voice is heard.
- Try breaking the group into pairs or trios to brainstorm *questions* on the topic rather than answers. Pairs or trios usually help the quiet members to be more active.

• Stand closer to the dominant talker since the presence of a facilitator will slow down the talker. If all else fails, placing your hand on the shoulder of a talker will silence that person. This is a last resort, of course.

Problems with Dependency

Signs of dependency include constant reference to the community builder and requests for decisions (rather than advice). Options for responses include:

• Rotate conveners, discussion leaders, or any role that can be identified. If necessary, co-leading the group helps model the behaviors you want to encourage.

• When leading a discussion, ask for comments from someone whose voice hasn't been heard yet.

• Try out different techniques for making decisions. Fist to Five uses hand signals (a fist is no agreement, five fingers raised is total agreement). Self-stick dots or markers for checks can be used to prioritize items.

• When extra information is needed, create a research team to identify and contact sources.

• When work involves writing and nobody will volunteer, ask for a helper to work with you or create a subcommittee to work with you on a draft.

Problems with the Disengaged

There's no way to build group capacity if members constantly drop out or refuse to engage in activities other than listening or criticizing. Here are some options for increasing commitment and activity:

• Check on the balance of task and maintenance. People will withdraw from a group if their needs for accomplishment (task) or socializing (maintenance) aren't being met.

• Have more fun and food. Include a pot luck dinner as part of a meeting or work session.

• Get some youth involved. Nothing improves the behavior of adults in a group more than having some kids present.

• Celebrate some successes to make sure everyone is aware of the progress that's being made.

• Find a friend in the media and make the group visible to the community. Photos, letters to the editor, feature stories, or radio call-in programs can be used this way.

From the Field

The Scenario

A small community (less than 500 people) located in a rather narrow valley wanted to modify its local land use plan to better conserve agricultural land and open spaces while still providing opportunities for residents to remain and find housing that is affordable to all economic groups. The community is strongly committed to these goals. The local planning commission wants to bring community members together to solicit their ideas on how the community should look ten years in the future. Community members are very involved in community activities, from painting the firehouse to building a community center to ensuring the continuation of the local elementary school. It is one of the most participatory communities in the county.

Tools and Techniques Used to Respond to the Issue

Using a grant from the state for municipal planning purposes, the town contracted with the regional planning commission to assist in a public forum that would provide information on a variety of housing programs as well as engage community members in a discussion about the town's future.

A meeting date was set; the local planning commission sent notices to every household in the community, which were followed up with selected telephone calls. The regional planning commission organized a panel of representatives of various housing organizations.

To encourage local involvement, the meeting was preceded by a potluck supper in the meeting room of the community church. Following the supper and the panel presentation, and a short break for more coffee and dessert, regional planning commission staff worked with community members on an exercise to solicit ideas about the community's future.

The process used was not unique but did encourage people who had lived in the community for some time to interact with others—in some cases for the first time. The commission staff did the following:

- Those present were asked to count out in eights (corresponding to the number of tables available).

- The groups were divided up by number (all the 1s at one table, the 2s at another, etc.). As it turned out—unplanned—there was a member of the local planning commission at each table.

- Each individual was asked to write on post-it notes one—and only one—thought about how they would like to see the town 10 years in the future. Each individual could provide multiple ideas but each had to be written on a separate post-it note.

- Participants were given 10 to 15 minutes to write down all of their ideas.

- Each participant, in turn, read one of their responses to the entire audience and posted it, randomly, on a large sheet near their table. The reading moved from table to table and participant to participant until all of the responses had been read and posted. This also included a table of younger children who had drawn pictures of their vision of the community.

- Each table then discussed—as a group—all of the responses that

could be consolidated, and came up with a final list. Each table's list was then shared with the entire group.

- The commission staff led a general discussion on the groups' reactions to what they had heard, asking for themes.

- The commission staff took the results of the evening and consolidated the group responses into a list of activities and goals to be brought back to the local planning commission.

- The planning commission went on to successfully revise the town plan and obtained another grant to bring the zoning and subdivision regulations into conformance with that plan.

Lessons Learned from the Development Experience

It seems obvious to say, but the most important lesson is that when people are involved in the creation of a product they will have greater ownership of the results.

Community character is an important component of a successful public involvement effort—particularly in activities that follow.

The more involvement there is from the local community in the planning of the event, the greater the likelihood of that event being successful.

Food helps!

—*Mark Blucher*
Vermont

Chapter Three
Issues, Goals and
a Vision of the Future

Much of the documentation of community activity over the last 50 years has as a major theme the issues, problems, crises or arguments that brought people together. Any type of activism, whether in the context of redistributing power or saving an historic courthouse, begins with the identification of an issue.

Identification can be considered both in the context of making a situation clear and getting to the heart of causes. But identification should also be considered as the way in which a topic—an issue—touches and changes a life. In other words, people who are brought into community leadership often identify WITH an issue. As a child, the great political activist, Elizabeth Cady Stanton, was found methodically cutting up a law text. She explained that she was going to get rid of the laws that made her father's legal clients cry. Now that's an early identification of and with an issue!

Goal setting in many ways is an extension of the identification process. This involves priorities and consensus and short and long-term results.

You might even consider issues, goals and a vision of the future to be the structure around which a community improvement plan is developed.

Why Bother?

When a community builder wonders about identifying issues, two rationales surface. The first is the focus that a specific topic offers to a work group. The second, selecting an issue to work on, is a process that helps recruit and motivate volunteers.

The identification of issues speaks to a common problem in communities—the multiple realities, rumors and theories that we all use to explain our world. Community builders must recognize that each group member has a personal perspective on local issues. Rarely does a group begin its work with shared understanding of circumstances already in place. Rather, that shared understanding is developed through the identification of issues and the research that's needed to make the situation clear.

The community builder's strategy certainly may use public opinion as a starting point, but part of the educational process is to search for alternative information, options, solutions, explanations that can fill out the simple picture. For example, one interpretation of a street with many abandoned vehicles is that the residents are lazy and don't take care of their cars. Another version might reflect the reality that if you can only buy a $500 car, it will break down and you won't be able to pay for repairs or towing. Yet another theory might be that there's no incentive to make a change (i.e., remove the cars) if there's no enforcement or assistance available to residents. Here, then, are three very different issues (lazy people, limited funds, no enforcement), all resulting from the same information (the abandoned cars). An outcome of working together to identify issues is the shared understanding that develops within the group.

Identification of issues is also a powerful recruiting tool. In many cases, the special interest folks who already have an agenda in mind will want to be part of the process. These folks will want to make sure that their perspective is heard and that they have some active role in decisions. On the other hand, once issues are identified, then the topic can be used to recruit people to participate because of that special topic. Many activists become skilled after involvement in a personal issue such as school quality or road improvement. Even elected officials are often attracted to public office because of a personal issue and then broaden their involvement.

Balancing Opinions and Data

Part of the identification of issues is, of course, dependent on information. At what point do opinions matter more than hard data? Many groups want validation for opinions only and don't really want to look at the results of data gathering or an environmental scan of the situation. Others see the compilation of facts and figures as much more significant than the collective wisdom and experience of any group.

It's definitely challenging for the community builder to balance the need for data and the need to honor opinions. This is a situation that calls for both qualitative and quantitative information. For example, by combining a desktop review of the numbers of pregnant girls under 18 in a county and the description of services provided with the results of a focus group of six or seven social workers and another of teen parents, a community builder should be able to paint a picture of what's going on

related to teen parenting. That's a combination of quantitative and qualitative information. Neither is more important and only in combination are they most useful.

Some groups will resist using anything other than their opinion. For them, the community builder has to find some compelling information that will inform their decision.

In every community there are people who will never have enough data. They will continue to survey, interview and read reports until the action-oriented folks have long since left the group. Identifying issues has to be handled as a snapshot approach to the current situation in a community in order to limit the data and opinion collection and not lose momentum. The snapshot idea, meaning that there's a picture of the situation/issue that's time specific, is one way to help the group move past infatuation with collecting data and on to the work of setting goals for improvement.

That Vision Thing

Some groups will spend an enormous amount of time creating a vision statement. However, this task can be accomplished in a limited amount of time with maximum involvement if the emphasis is placed on words or phrases rather than a fully crafted vision. Individuals and small groups can offer words or phrases and then a subcommittee or trio can wordsmith a draft statement. The review and revision of the draft statement is vital to create acceptance.

Perhaps even more important than how the vision statement is created is how it's used during the rest of a community betterment project. Is the vision of the ideal, preferred future the reference point for setting goals and taking action? That is, does the group constantly ask, Will this proposed goal (strategy, action) get us closer to our vision? The vision statement as reference point can't be overemphasized. It can also be used as a tool to deal with conflict with the same type of questioning strategy.

Inventing new ways to share the vision statement can also be a fun way to involve the more creative members of a group. Communities have printed their vision statement on business cards, made posters or held elementary school art contests around their vision.

Shared Goals

Community builders use a number of tried and true methods to arrive at shared goals. The emphasis, of course, is on the consensus that emerges when goals are shared. That consensus becomes the glue that holds the group together. Discussing issues and narrowing down the topics that can be addressed by the group naturally leads to setting some goals related to change. This is the expected response to the discussion of what's wrong or needs to be changed in a community setting.

There are some notable processes that can help ensure success in goal development. First, there should be some context for the goals. This might include discussion and identification of issues or a SWOT (strengths, weaknesses, opportunities and threats) analysis. The context might also be a list of assets or strengths related to an issue. However framed, the context creates some boundaries for goals rather than opening up the entire universe of topics.

Secondly, if a previous plan or project offers some history, the work of the past should be brought into the conversation about goals. Revise existing goals if there's still work to be done. Third, there should be some type of public process for selecting priorities among goals. In a public meeting session, self-adhesive dots can be used and participants can demonstrate their choices for immediate compilation. Simple check marks can work in the same way. The important part of this is the narrowing of choices so that a few strategic goals are selected and then the group proceeds towards some action.

Community Builder Strategies

1. Keep After the Real Issues

Try to avoid simplistic thinking about complicated issues. The first answer might not be the right answer, so don't be fearful of pushing the group to get to the core issue. One good technique to use is to keep asking Why? or Why does that happen/exist? It's part of the community builder's role to help the group get past superficial answers to real issues. Here's an example: When discussing school vandalism, some group members blame new migrants in town because their kids roam the streets after school. Is the issue bad parenting? Or lack of after-school services? Or perhaps problems getting access to information about programs?

2. Anyone Can Be a Researcher

With today's Internet access, almost any community group member can research a topic, find examples from other towns or contact state and federal agencies. Use the curiosity and interest of the group to educate everyone by recruiting members to find out facts and background on issues.

3. Look at Sample Vision Statements

It's not a bad idea to offer some sample vision statements from other towns, organizations or businesses. Many people work best if they have a model rather than trying to deal with an abstract, vaguely defined product.

4. There are Slogans and Then There are Vision Statements

Many communities or organizations will create a paragraph vision statement that describes the future they prefer and then also have a tag line or slogan for their community. This is a chance to use a one-line sentence or phrase that really identifies the community. The one-line version is also much better for marketing and publicity purposes.

5. What's a Mission Statement?

Lots of community builders and volunteers will confuse a vision statement with the mission statement. While there are many definitions, one way to look at the difference is that the vision statement deals with the ideal or preferred future and the mission statement deals with purpose, audience and procedures.

6. Issue, Vision, Goal— They Fit Together Like a Russian Doll

An excellent explanation of how this all fits together is a reference to the Russian doll that contains a smaller version of itself inside. The issue is the core, the vision is the next layer, then the goal statements and so on…. Any way that you can translate these abstract ideas for the concrete thinkers will be helpful. Sometimes the analogy of a jigsaw puzzle can be helpful, too.

Troubleshooting

Here are some common problems encountered by community builders in identifying issues, creating vision statements and setting shared goals.

They've Already Got an Agenda

It's not uncommon to face an organized small group that has a special agenda within the larger community group. These folks can tilt the process and make their own interests seem most important.

- Expand the group. Adding more people will change the balance of power within the group.
- Make good use of trios, pairs or table group discussions to get everyone to participate.
- Ask for more information and assign pairs to do some research and come back to the group.
- Use the dot activity or some other priority selection technique to give everyone an equal chance to select topics.
- Create a place on the agenda for lobbying and contain the folks with an agenda to just one part of the meeting

We've Done This Before

Because this type of planning is so important, many group members will already have some experience with the process of visioning and creating goals. That's not necessarily bad and can even be an advantage, unless the experience was really negative and you have to deal with the aftermath.

- Try to make your process a bit different by translating jargon into everyday language.
- Use anything you can think of to break up the monotony of a meeting. Try food, kids offering entertainment, door prizes, or guest speakers (only if they are really good) to make the experience different.
- When all else fails, resort to your champion or someone credible in the community to promote participation, extend invitations and send thank yous for helping.
- Refer back to the experienced folks as experts. Ask them to compare their experience with what's going on at the work session. (Fred, how did your bank

handle the environmental scan and identifying issues?)

All We Do Is Talk

Spending too much time on the discussion of issues, setting goals and creating a vision statement can be very tough for the concrete thinkers who are action oriented. If you notice some decline in attendance, it may be these folks who have stopped coming to the work sessions.

- Try involvement in data collection or research. Asking group members to do two or three interviews, some Internet research or help with a survey can provide some action steps that will keep people involved.
- Use small groups or subcommittees to draft the vision statement and let the large group review it with suggestions for revisions. This will make the process go faster.
- Get some publicity for the content of your discussions. Even a letter to the editor or an opinion editorial can turn the abstract into a concrete product for the public eye.
- Broaden the discussion to include a youth perspective.

Most community projects are short on young participants. Invite a high school class to join the group.

I'd Rather Eat a Spider than Do Another Survey

How many times has the community been the subject of a survey? When was the most recent survey done? Have the results ever been used or even discussed? Sometimes the only way to get quantitative information is to conduct some type of survey, but overcoming local resistance can be quite a challenge.

- Get some professional help. Community colleges can be a good source of assistance through teachers and classes. Consider a small grant to help pay costs for involvement in design and delivery of a survey.
- Use kids up front as interviewers or to deliver surveys. Another great source of labor are Eagle Scouts looking for community projects. Why spend their energy painting benches when they can deliver or compile surveys?
- Consider electronic surveys. You might be surprised at the low cost of paying a service to manage e-mail surveys for you.

- Make sure you use whatever already exists. If a survey is less than three years old, it's worth discussing the results.
- Use simple summaries to get folks to look at the results. Three to five major points in a newspaper or church bulletin article can help get the information out.
- Try selecting some results for a True/False test for a service club as a way to get folks interested in the results.

From the Field

The Scenario

In February of 1999, the citizens of Morrilton, Arkansas (population 6,470) saw two major employers close their doors within a one-week period, displacing nearly 1,100 workers. How does a small community, in a small rural county, cope with the wholesale decimation of the workforce? Conway County was as ready as a rural area could be. Their history—900 jobs lost in 1985 when a cotton plant closed—combined with the inspiration of a few key leaders, moved them to form the Conway County Vision 2020 Leadership Institute in 1995. In 1996, the community adopted VISION 2010 as a component of

their Vision 2020 effort. VISION 2010 is partnership initiative coordinated by the Cooperative Extension Service with the goal of Building Healthy Sustainable Communities for the 21st Century. A steering committee and leadership team were formed to participate in seven VISION 2010 seminars dealing with topics of strategic visioning and planning, education, workforce preparation, economic development, leadership development, facilitation skills, sustaining the development process—all with a focus on the knowledge-based economy.

Tools and Techniques Used to Respond to the Issue

A team of leaders attended the first VISION 2010 Seminar—on strategic visioning—that led them to one of their first major projects. The community raised $100,000 within a three-day window in order to purchase and launch MAST (Morrilton's Association with Spatial Technology) technology lab. The money was matched 3.5 to 1, giving the community a $450,000 lab. The goal of this learning laboratory is for youth to learn technology while working on projects that benefit the community.

VISION 2010's leadership team found an ideal way to involve youth in contributing to their future. To identify their common vision for the future, leaders participating in the leadership institute paired up and went to all corners of the county to survey residents. A conscious decision was made to gather qualitative, rather than quantitative, information. The survey forms asked open questions. The teens in the MAST lab compiled data from over 1600 surveys. The shared vision formed the core of the action plan developed by the VISION 2010 action teams.

One advantage of a common vision for the community is the ability to act quickly when opportunities arise that are consistent with that vision. When a commercial fitness center closed down, Morrilton leaders seized the opportunity to acquire a large facility to develop a community center. For $250,000, the Morrilton area now enjoys the community center valued at $1.1 million.

Lessons Learned from the Development Experience

- Being proactive about community, leadership and economic development is important in a dynamic economy environment.
- Establishing a county leadership institute created a cadre of people who were knowledgeable, skilled, and had a high trust level with each other.
- Before beginning a new program like VISION 2010, it is critical to discuss how that program can support and complement what is already happening in the community.
- People volunteer because they are asked. Personal contact is critical.
- The change of attitude—from we can't do it to we can do anything—is the most important impact of the Conway County Vision 2020 Leadership Institute.
- Even though layoffs were not a surprise in Conway County, the effect was considerable.
- Creative use of resources is essential. For example, using the school computer labs to train displaced workers in non-school

hours made use of an underutilized asset.

- Conway County leaders excel in casting a broad net for resources outside the community. Examples include VISION 2010, University of Arkansas Cooperative Extension Service, the local electric utility (ENTERGY), the Arkansas Department of Economic Development, the Institute for Economic Advancement at the University of Arkansas-Little Rock, and the Arkansas Department of Workforce Education.
- Seize the moment! As opportunities arise while strategic

visioning is in progress, it is important not to wait for a completed plan to be written.

- The plan is important, but the process of planning through citizen involvement is more important than a completed document.
- A separate writing team (for the plan) is helpful in freeing study action teams to focus on critical issues.
- One wise Conway County leader recommends the Nine Ps for Progress. They include: Plan, People, Professional Assistance, Potential, Perception, Patience, Perseverance, Publicity and Prayer.

—*Mark Peterson*
Arkansas

Chapter Four

Vision to Action

Making Progress

Community builders need many skills, types of knowledge, and positive attitudes. The later comes in handy especially when many barriers exist. Human nature seldom lives up to the ideal. Discouragement can appear like Kirkegaard's famous abyss. Sometimes, it's very important to be able to know if the long hours and hard work have actually made a difference.

This is one point in any community project when making the transition from vision to action is crucial. Even the most positive person needs the encouragement of seeing action steps and results. Don't underestimate the importance of this to your own motivation. Taking action is also motivational for community groups, too.

Many groups can work together to identify issues and set shared goals but fail in this transition from the abstract to the concrete. As noted in other chapters, the action-oriented volunteers are put off by future talk, strategy sessions and long discussions. By this point, they might have even left the group. A longtime friend of the Heartland Center, Nette Nelson, used to tell the story of two vultures sitting in a tree endlessly waiting. Finally one said to the other, "I can't stand this. Let's go kill something!" Is the level of frustration over lack of action in your community group that high? Maybe it's time to turn the focus toward short-term, tangible results.

Why Bother?

Aside from personal satisfaction in seeing process turn into product, there is another issue that the vision to action transition will address: credibility. This means credibility of the community project, the members of the group and most certainly of the community builder herself.

Have you personally been part of a group that never accomplished anything? Or know a group that was stalled on some planning stage or trapped by interpersonal conflict? Getting to the point of action and results is what gives credibility and meaning to all those involved. Meaningful participation requires action. Public credibility demands action and results. So, some dimension of the rationale for making sure projects get to the action phase has to do with personal fulfillment and the public response.

There is a basic, common sense reason why vision has to be translated into action. We'd all eventually run into severe job criticism if we didn't have some proof of action in our community building work. We'd be unable to justify employment or consulting contracts if we didn't help the group get to the point of

taking action.

Consider the classic definition of community development, long held by the International Community Development Society: Community development means purposive change. The definition used by the Heartland Center is:

Community development (community building) happens when a group in a locality initiates a planned process to change the economic, social, cultural or environmental situation. Change equals action in the community equation.

Accountability

Naturally, there are many levels of accountability. Filling out time sheets, tracking billable hours, comparing progress to a timeline—these all are methods for dealing with accountability. The area that is most frequently forgotten, however, is the accountability to the larger community (rather than the funding source!).

One way to address public accountability is to make sure that the project has high visibility within the community. Rather than reporting just to a funding source, an administrative authority, or an elected body, this approach involves marketing strategies that place the project on a much higher visibility level.

Many community builders enjoy good relationships with local media contacts and manage to get their project stories on the radio and in the paper quite often. Developing strategies that include all types of outlets from church bulletins to high school web pages requires effort but really pays off in terms of visibility.

This type of high profile builds in public accountability and can serve as an insurance policy against last minute naysayers. If there's been news about the project in many forms, it's much easier to cope with criticism as the project progresses.

Maintaining Momentum

Keeping adequate numbers of volunteers in a project is perhaps the most basic challenge of community building. Constraints on time, competition with other community activities and life in general prevent many volunteers from even starting involvement. All the same issues, of course, tend to push volunteers away from commitments.

However, the best response to lack of interest and commitment is getting to the action stage quickly and showing some immediate results. More people can be recruited by one highly visible community work session than hundreds of flyers and posters. Habitat For Humanity, for example, uses this approach to recruit volunteers to help with building projects. People are intrigued and attracted by activity. This is why community clean-up projects are so often the beginning of an entire series of community projects.

Pay Attention to Strategies and Techniques

1. Small Tasks are Only Whelming, not Overwhelming

While some action steps can seem too big to tackle, small tasks are hard to refuse. A volunteer might actually run from the room if asked to initiate research on home ownership of abandoned buildings but would agree to make three phone calls. The smaller and more specific, the more likely the assignment will be accepted.

2. Use the Buddy System When Possible

Asking two people to help each other with a task makes perfect sense. Not only will they offer each other support, but they are much more likely to remind each other to get to work on their assignment.

3. Make the Names and Dates Public

Use newsprint or email to publicize the Who will do What by When information of an action plan. Verbal agreement is fine, but in our western culture, seeing names and deadlines in writing makes an important impact on people. It solidifies a verbal yes or a head nod and lets the entire group in on the assignment.

4. Try a Room Size Time Line

Newsprint can also be used horizontally to make a project time line extend around the room at eye level. An excellent group activity is completing the time line. The time line may even start sometime in the past and note important events that created the current situation.

5. Don't Miss a Single Chance to Market

Church bulletins, radio call-in shows, storefront posters, children's art contests, senior citizen flyers, place mats at the local café are all ways to market a project and raise the visibility of the community effort. Sometimes the very best ideas in this area can come from a mixed age group that's brainstorming all the ways people in town find out about news. One important addition to any list are the five or six important people to tell who will make sure everyone else knows what's going on.

6. Celebrate Lots of Things

Along with the added visibility and satisfaction of completing small steps toward a community goal, the element of celebration can be very useful to the community builder. Go back to the time line and celebrate with food and applause the completion of a step in the action plan. Don't be afraid that you'll celebrate too much, or that the group will think you are foolish for wanting to applaud members who made phone calls or got out a mailing. Make the celebration sincere.

Troubleshooting

Here are some typical problems that a community builder might encounter when moving a group from vision to action.

But I've Always Done This Part

Ever faced a person or service club that wants to do just one task and won't let anyone help? This can be a stalemate in the vision to action transition.

- Make sure you're giving due credit. Recognition can go a long way to helping folks see how their long-time contribution fits into the action plan.
- Along those same lines, try to expand the task or make it larger in order to demonstrate how it fits into the action plan.
- See if the territorial behavior can be turned into a mentoring or training attitude. Asking a person to help train others in his skills is very flattering.
- When in doubt, reframe! There are times when a community tradition—such as a pancake feed or event—originated as a response to a particular issue or question. Try reframing the event in terms of new issues and situations, and see if that attracts new helpers.

We Can't Do Anything Without a Grant

Apathy can become contagious and this excuse can sound like a Greek chorus that drowns out any good ideas for action. All you need is one highly credible person in town to start saying this, and momentum will be in danger.

- Offer examples from other towns and areas to show that a lot can be done that doesn't require outside funding. Examples should come from somewhat similar places so that the message is clear—if they can do this, so can we.
- Review history of what's been done before. If you can find motivating examples from your own community, all the better.
- Talk about first steps and phases. Maybe outside funding will be needed eventually, but there's always something that can be done here and now and

by local folks.

- Don't be afraid to confront. If all else fails, refer back to the questions, If not now, when? And If not us, then who?

Sure We Missed the Meetings, but We Can Still Complain

When naysayers come late to the project and begin to complain or criticize, it's hard to keep from asking where they've been all along! However, this type of late criticism can be avoided.

- Make the process as public as possible. Use all those media outlets and individuals to get people talking and listening.

- Try starting each work session with a 30-minute update session and ask group members to take turns talking to newcomers before the real work session begins. This way, new folks can be brought into the group at any point.

- Develop a 30-second sound bite for everyone in the group as a response to criticism. Agree on the language and the message and let everyone practice in pairs at least once. That way, when they encounter criticism, they'll have a starting point for discussion.

From the Field

The Scenario

With 4H becoming more volunteer led than ever before in Alabama, I have been faced with the problem of getting volunteers to lead or actively participate in different aspects of many of the programs that we have going on in the county. And without volunteers the 4H program in my area would come to a near standstill.

Tools or Techniques Used to Respond to the Issue

Most people you'll come in contact with can be classified as one-timers, meaning you can easily convince them to participate in a program or activity one time, but it is nearly impossible to get them to commit on a regular basis. That's okay, because from this pool of one-timers you will gradually find people who are willing to commit more of their time to different programs.

One-timers can be anyone. I often recruit police officers, parents, lawyers, bankers, schoolteachers, firefighters, nurses, doctors and business owners. The list can go on and on. And usually when I do use a one-timer, I will have them fill out a list of other interests or hobbies they might have, that I can then place in a file for future use. I keep a file of peoples' interests because I never know when I'm doing a program or activity that someone might have as a hobby or interest and would be more than happy to participate in. Remember people are most willing to donate their time to things they are passionate about, and the trick is finding what those interests are.

For example, I wanted a fire fighter to come to a club meeting to speak to the children about fire safety and fire hazards. I went to the local fire department and asked around and shortly found a firefighter who could come on our meeting day. After the meeting, I asked if he would fill out a form listing some interest, hobbies and passions of his,

which he did very quickly. About four months later, some kids wanted to learn how to do woodworking. I browsed through the files of people I had on record and discovered that the firefighter I used once before did woodworking in his spare time. I contacted him and he agreed to meet with that group of kids every other week, teaching them good woodworking skills. By keeping a record of interest of that person, he now is a 4H volunteer leader of a woodworking club.

Lessons Learned from the Development Experience

Don't try forcing a person to volunteer all their time to a project. That's the quickest way to drive a person away. Instead, use them once or twice, keeping a record of their personal interests. And if the occasion ever arises where your program and their interests coincide, then give them a call. Most of the time, they will be willing to help out again or even take the lead. Discovering the interests of people can be a great way to build up a volunteer base a community.

— *Carl Hughes*
Alabama

Chapter Five
Finding the $$$
to Make Things Happen

Many community projects are stalled at birth because people believe there are no resources available or that finding resources and writing grants is too complicated and competitive. Nothing can be farther from the truth. There is a lot of money out there, and, given the aging of the baby boomers, the massive wealth transfer predicted for the first half of the century means there will be even more money available.

True, grant writing is a craft that requires both skills and creativity, but more importantly, people find resources when they believe in what they are doing and are committed to making things happen. Sometimes those resources come from within the community rather than result from grant writing. Sometimes the resources flow from a partnership with another organization. Community builders interested in helping communities find resources need to look at the whole funding picture including: (1) fee for service, which requires the group to identify what skills, products and services they have that others will pay to access; (2) fundraising events, which range from providing a service, to selling pancakes at the fair, to seeking donations; (3) partnerships with existing organizations that can extend their services to meet the desired goals; (4) for-profit ventures that support non-profit programs; and (5) grant writing. Communities that want to build and support new long-term efforts usually have to rely on most or all of the strategies to develop a long-range funding plan.

Why Bother?

Ultimately, those communities that successfully transition into the 21st century will all have mastered the art and craft of finding resources. Often their efforts will rely on grant funding to get started, but for the long haul they will branch into other forms of fundraising.

Fundraising, like other skills in this field guide, is a skill that can be learned. Fundraising is also an arena where groups can utilize the diverse talents of their group in concert. For example, someone who enjoys being up front and doing marketing can make the in-person pitches. Your quiet introvert, who enjoys the Internet, can research options and background. Your yet-unpublished author can craft the proposals. Successful fundraising is a team sport.

Community groups seem to break along a clear divide—those that are getting money and support and those that talk about not knowing how to get money. People speak of lucky breaks. And, indeed, fundraising is an area rife with lucky breaks. Those who succeed in the long run are those who build on their lucky breaks to create a system for group or community fundraising.

Understand the System

Successful community builders know that in the long run, it is what the community or group does for itself that matters. Outsiders don't solve our problems; we do. So, the first rule is to see outside resources as only one of many tools your community or group will use to implement the vision. Acquainting yourselves with other similar groups or communities who are successful in accessing funding can help you see what needs to be in place for your group or community to succeed.

When we look at funders, we need to be aware that most giving results from individual people reaching into their pockets and giving to something they believe in. These pockets, inside your community or outside, constitute the largest pool of available funds. People give to people and in many ways.

Second, the federal government offers many opportunities for communities and groups to request funding. Generally, those seeking these funds are governmental units or non-profits. The federal government must publish notice of these opportunities and does so in the Federal Register or, less frequently, the Commerce Daily. The Catalogue of Federal Domestic Assistance (http://www.cfda.gov/) provides a general guide to federal grantmaking, listing all programs in statute, which means you need to check to see if there is funding appropriated.

Third, foundations provide grants and contracts to communities and groups to apply for funding. To be eligible, the asking group must have a not-for-profit status. Finally, many corporations have foundations or giving programs which are often tied to location and may be geared to furthering corporate goals. For example, pharmaceutical companies often give to health-related research or patient education. A few hours on the Internet can easily net opportunities in all of the last three categories.

Examine Attitudes in Your Group and Community

Because it is so very easy to find some potential sources, lack of knowledge is an excuse that hides the real reason why some groups don't move forward with their fundraising goals. Just wanting something doesn't position you to get money. People get money because they have a well-thought out plan. So, the first thing to work on is getting your group or community to move from wishing to planning—detailed planning that includes the who, what and when. Occasionally, the planning process leads to the conclusion that everything needed is already available, it just needs to be mobilized. Having a draft plan in hand means that someone looking at a funding opportunity can see how to respond to the application guidelines rather than stare at the form without a starting point. The Grantsmanship Center likens the grant writing process to a clock. Preparation to write the grant occupies the first seven hours on the clock, the writing two additional hours, and post submission activity the last three hours.

A second very important attitudinal shift requires the group or community to look at fundraising from a marketing perspective. Often, we seek funding based on the fact that our community is so poor, our youth so at risk, or our environment so fragile. Funders want to help, but not because you are the worst off. They want to help because you have the best solution; a solution that you can share with others and that makes them know that their money was used wisely. Take a marketing approach and focus on what the funder is buying—successful solutions. To successfully market your idea to funders, you must be very clear about the product you want them to buy—your plan. What need of theirs does it address? How do the characteristics of your plan line up with their guidelines and selection criteria? In addition to the project for which you are seeking funding, your product package also includes your mission and vision statements, your organizational needs assessment or strategic plan, your history and partners, and your reputation. Your community or group may wish to evaluate its strengths, weaknesses, opportunities, and threats in the context of searching for funding.

A good marketing plan also requires us to look at the competition. Who else is seeking similar funding? Who else addresses the same need? This information will help you determine how you are different from the competition, something that makes your request special. Analyzing this information can help you determine how you fit into the overall scheme of things and what characteristics make your group or community stand out from the rest. This process may also lead you to uncover some weaknesses. Perhaps you can improve your positioning by building bridges with other organizations. Clearly understanding what makes your project unique will assist you in sifting through all the possibilities to target those potential funders whose missions are congruent with yours and whose focuses match that of your community or group. This process may also lead you to refine, modify, or even substantially change your original plan.

Who You Know

Fundraising is one area where the abstract concept of social capital makes a real difference. People say we are all only six contacts away from the President or the Pope. Organizations that want to succeed in accessing outside resources must take their bridging social capital (links to organizations and individuals external to our group, linked either horizontally to similar groups or vertically to other types of groups with similar focus) very seriously. They need to find the three contacts between their organization and key funders or opinion makers.

If government funding plays a big role in the future of your project, it is time to become well acquainted with your congressional delegation and staff, state agency staff, and/or Tribal government officials. Similarly, if you plan to rely on religion-based funding, you and members of your group should have many significant contacts. If you plan on raising your funds from the private sector, you will need to have those contacts securely in your pocket.

In making overtures to your new network partners, try a value-added approach where you bring something of value to them such as contact with their constituency, new information, or program results of interest. Once you begin making these contacts, your valuable connections back to the community will lead you to additional partners and supporters. One tip to remember in making these contacts is that board members and volunteers make a more favorable first impression since staff can be seen as trying to save their job rather than address a community problem. Staff can then follow up on the contact.

Pay Attention to Strategies and Techniques

1. Follow the Guidelines Exactly and Carefully

Many newcomers to the funding game find that their project is just a bit off the guidelines, or they already have something written and decide it's not worth it to rewrite to match the criteria. Foundation officers have described themselves as cranky when they receive applications that don't follow the guidelines exactly

and carefully. One of the last things you want to do is get someone cranky because we all remember people who make us cranky. And, funders talk to each other—a lot; your cranky program officer could tell staffers from 10 other organizations how cranky you made them. Remember also that deadlines are deadlines, period.

2. Specifically Address the Funders' Mission or Selection Criteria

When you send something into a funder you want to do everything possible to make it easy for them to give you lots of points or good comments. To that end, one trick is to take the guidelines, purpose and selection criteria and highlight all the key ideas and phrases. In grant writing it is a good idea to use the same terminology as the funder. While you might focus on at-risk youth, the funder may speak about resilient youth. You want to use their terminology to demonstrate that you have read and understood their information and that you are coming from the same place. Use this information to generate an outline that follows the criteria or guidelines, plugging in information about your project in the appropriate place.

3. Hook the Reader

Remember that people give to people, even in the foundation and government-funding world. Just as they estimate that people assess a resume in the first seven seconds they look at it, readers of your request will make a judgment in the first 60 seconds they look at it. What first meets the eye should capture their attention. Good use of white space, type font, and graphics can help. Some writers hook their readers by starting with a key quote, poem, headline, or case study—something that gets their attention.

4. Collaboration

Today almost all funders look at who the partners are in any project and the degree of partner involvement. Years ago, we could get by with a list or partners. We used support letters that commented on what good folks we were, what great work we did, and how everybody wanted to see the project succeed. This evidence of support is generally not worth the paper it is written on. Funders want to see meaningful collaboration, which means commitment of resources to help the project succeed. Creative grant writers can develop great matrices of partners, their contribution, and the link back to the project goals by counting on partners who help publicize, host, or help with events, for example.

5. The Importance of Significance

Many funders will ask the writer to address the project's potential significance. Often writers respond with several general statements about how important they see the project. Such an approach misses a key opportunity to ensure your proposal rises to the top. Remember, funders are interested in buying ideas that further the mission and goals of their organizations. Addressing significance is where you make the case that your project will give them their money's worth and more.

One way to address the significance of your project is to look at it in terms of levels. One level is how the project will be significant to those directly impacted (perhaps those who receive some type of service, for example). A second level addresses those impacted indirectly, through system improvement or related impacts such as lowered

taxes or greater safety. A third level speaks to the community builders and the field of work. How you address significance shapes your response to the question about dissemination. The funder can then see how your grant will have a broad impact beyond the boundaries of your community.

6. Communications is Key

Many grant writers think they are done when they hit the send button or dump the request in the mail. Not a chance! Good grant writers and fundraisers know this is the time to take a deep breath and begin the thank you letters. Once you receive word on the outcome, it is time for another round of communications to let everyone know the results. Today we can put these names on an e-list and keep our supporters well connected throughout the project or to the next request. Don't forget the funder, who should receive a thank you regardless of the outcome. Once you are funded, you want to maintain regular communication. Your program officer, whenever possible, should be part of your team. One strategy is to send them a post card after major meetings.

Troubleshooting

Brainstorming to Get Started

Sometimes the most difficult step is the first one. Groups have trouble moving from we want this to a proposal that addresses why it is needed and what the outcomes will be. One way to get started on drafting a request is to work with your group brainstorming answers to the following questions:

- What do we want to do?
- Why?
- Why would people care about what we want to do?

Following the brainstorming ask people to come up with:

- A one sentence solution
- Three activities to make the project work
- Five ways to know we are successful

Overcoming the Blank Screen Syndrome

Even when you worked on the plan it is all too easy to find yourself without a starting point on the actual writing of the proposal. There is nothing more debilitating than sitting at the computer looking at a blank screen with no idea how to get started.

- One strategy is to develop an outline and use it.
- Write something, *anything*, that relates to the proposal. Put down your thoughts on where the idea came from, or make up a scenario of how it would work if funded. You can use pieces like this eventually.
- Enter key phrases, selection criteria and other thoughts on topics that need to be included. You may find yourself already on page three!
- Start with a piece that you know how to do. Are you a good budget creator? Do that. Good at creating short biographies from long resumes? Do that.
- List everyone who's been part of the process to develop the ideas, then create a timeline of how it all came to this point. This history can be useful and it'll get you started on thinking and writing.

Nobody Wants to Take the Lead

What happens when there's interest all along and then everyone declines? If nobody wants to step up and start grant writing or preparing materials for fundraising, here are some ideas.

- Make it a team sport and use brainstorming to get ideas recorded.
- Divide the work into sections and recruit helpers to draft each part.
- Assemble a review team of your own to read the proposal with a scoring sheet and make suggestions.

- Do a short, small special fundraiser to hire a writer. Gather folks together, state the case and ask them to get their checkbooks out to help.

Jump While You Can

It is not uncommon for people to develop serious concerns about a fundraising effort half way into the effort. Better to stop and regroup than to go forward when the time and team aren't right. Other opportunities will evolve.

From the Field

The Scenario

In June 2000, our team received a $15,000 grant to form a business incubation center to address southern Illinois Perry County's continuing loss of businesses and jobs. The first issue we faced was the development of the incubation center facility and its program. We had learned of business incubators in workshops, but no one on the team had coursework in or experience with the incubator concept. There is no Chamber of Commerce or business development organization in southern Perry County. From statistics gathered during the writing of our grant, we knew we had few local resources to help us. The communities of southern Perry County have been classified as pockets of poverty. The community has few professionals beyond the educators in the school system. Most of these professionals live outside the area. Our southern Perry County community could not provide the educational or financial resources we needed to start a business incubation center.

Tools or Techniques Used to Respond to the Issue

To develop a business incubation center in this impoverished environment, we needed to seek resources and assistance from outside the area. We turned to regional and state economic development agencies. The following is a list of our most successful resources:

- ACEnet, the Appalachian Center for Economic Networks, helped us organize our objectives and develop a plan of action. ACEnet awarded us a $10,000 grant in August 2001 for program and staff development. Through ACEnet we learned of an Ohio Community Computing Center Network (OCCN) grant and have collaborated with two other local groups to obtain a grant for a community computer technology center which will contain a business development hub.
- Small Business Development Center representatives have provided us with materials and training classes, computer programs, contact names, and con-

ference and grant information.

- The Governor's Office of Appalachia regional office has helped us obtain an Ohio Planning Grant to conduct a community assessment survey.
- An Ohio State University Agricultural Extension Economic Development Agent has included us in a government grant the Extension Service is writing. One of our members serves on this board.
- Appalachian New Economy Partnerships (ANEP) has selected us as a pilot project for an Access Ohio initiative that proposes to place a fast Internet infrastructure in rural Appalachian communities to encourage economic growth.
- The Appalachian Roundtable and Access Appalachia conferences put us in contact with individuals who can help us find computer technology businesses, locate funding for potential businesses and provide e-commerce instruction. We learned of the Foundation of Appalachian Ohio during these conferences and have applied for a grant to develop a Community Asset Building

Initiative to conduct after-school entrepreneurship classes and assist and encourage students to use their computer-related skills to produce marketable products and services and start a business—to become entrepreneurs.

- The Internet has proven to be a valuable information-gathering and timesaving tool. The National Business Association and the National Business Incubation Association have good websites.

Lessons Learned from this Development Experience

The circles of contacts and resources grow in a ripple effect. Locating and developing resources will be a basic and ongoing part of the incubation center's business assistance process. We know the time spent in meetings, classes and conferences is necessary if we are to improve our expertise and enlarge our network of resources. Working with these resources has made our group a stronger, more accountable organization, brought state and regional attention to our efforts, and leveraged additional funding. SBDC personnel, their organizations and the regional and state economic development agencies have been willing and enthusiastic supporters of our efforts in southern Perry County, Ohio.

—Lilian Winnenberg
Ohio

Chapter Six
Evaluation for Survival and Success

How Do You Know if What You're Doing Works?

Everyone wants to do work that is worthwhile. For those of us who have been engaged in community building for most of our careers, we're also thinking in terms of legacy or what we might leave behind us for others. As difficult as community building can be, the knowledge that our efforts have made a positive difference is the underlying motivation that keeps us on task. Sometimes we need to be reminded of that larger picture of contribution just so that we don't forget that we're in this work for the long term. Making a difference is certainly important to community volunteers, too, in terms of both recruitment and continuing involvement.

So how do we find out if what we're doing works? How do we find time to reflect on progress? How do we stop action long enough to consider alternatives? Evaluation... outcomes...impacts...indicators...measurements...these are all terms that can give a community builder an instant headache! Of course we know it's important, but isn't this type of reflection usually the last thing we build into a community betterment project? This chapter deals with some ways to avoid the headache and embrace the importance of keeping track of the effort in a way that's useful and practical.

Why Bother?

Sometimes, you have to evaluate or track success in order to receive funding for a project. Sometimes, you have to measure success in order to prove your (or the project's) worth or to justify your existence. In other words, keeping track of results can be a survival issue. With that in mind, the context or purpose has to be the framework we consider first of all. Is this an externally imposed, required reporting step? Is there a format already in place? Is this simply a reporting function that will rely on the time honored body count approach (i.e., counting how many folks attended meetings)? Do you need numbers and success stories to avoid a budget cut or reduction in force? Or is evaluation/success a means to keep political forces on your side or at least at bay for a while? None of these circumstances is unusual.

Perhaps, in addition to the necessity, there are some options built into the need for evaluation. Is there an opportunity for honest improvement? Can part of the evaluation be done as the project moves along and provide feedback to be used for a midpoint correction? Evaluations can be summative: documentation of process, involvement, and plan that sums up the work. Evaluations can also be formative: conducted at regular intervals so that the information can interact with the project and allow for adjustments, corrections and new ideas. Both approaches are valuable and not at all mutually exclusive. It's a question of timing and the use

of the information that's gathered.

The most interesting work that's been done recently with evaluation concepts has developed from Peter Senge's work on the so-called learning community. The idea here is that a team, an organization or a community work group can establish an environment in which a regular process for reflection and learning replaces the end of the project evaluation. Developing specific learning questions that focus reflection on the audience to be served and the desired outcome gives some structure, but the true learning comes from the regular review with the feedback information. It's not just asking How are we doing? but pausing to figure out what the answer really means and what the implications are for procedures, organization, delivery and continuation.

In the world of community building, there's a lot to learn from evaluation efforts and trying to measure success. Another wonderful source of information for improving comes from the examples of other community projects. The field trip to visit a town with similar issues and projects can do a lot to energize a group, avoid pitfalls, and apply new ideas to the effort at hand.

Internet research can provide any number of contacts and information about community projects that might offer some good advice.

Let Them Do It

Along with the theme of creating an environment within the community group that eagerly learns from evaluation feedback, there's a theme of participation that has emerged from international rural development. Participatory evaluation is an approach that relies on the community builder to help structure an evaluation and share skills that are needed to collect and analyze information. The actual work, as the term implies, is done by the participants themselves

Evaluation is often seen as a process that is done *to* people rather than *with or by* people as in participatory evaluation. One way to look at this method is to consider who the question makers are. If the evaluation questions come from inside the project, that's probably a good sign that it's a participatory process.

In this approach, group members decide not only what questions to ask but what success will look like based on the goals they set. For example, if club members decide

that more financial organization is needed and a budget retreat is set for the board, then perhaps success in this case will be a process for every committee to use in spending the club's money, an increase in club dues and new fundraising events held.

This approach has so much potential for learning new skills and for improving the project because of the participation from start to finish.

But Can We Measure Success?

In recent years, a great deal has been written about indicators and measurement of success. Several large communities such as Seattle have developed indicators and measures of preserving quality of life and the environment. Sometimes, though, when a community builder looks at a large project, it's difficult to make the translation to the scale of a small community or a betterment project. At first view, the idea of measuring progress can seem so daunting that many community builders avoid it entirely.

Another pitfall in the measurement game is selecting a change that doesn't tell us the whole story. For example, a goal for economic development might be to create more jobs. We can count the current number of jobs and measure the change over time. But what if the jobs that are created pay only the minimum wage and have no health benefits, thereby forcing more families to rely on public assistance programs?

Through thoughtful discussion of the issue, development of a vision and reaching shared goals, the group can select what to measure. And the very first step is to define a baseline that describes the current situation. For a goal such as "Engage more youth in community betterment projects," the *baseline* might be the current number of participants under 18 in all community service clubs. An *indicator* of progress would be an increase in youth participants. After identifying some actions for recruitment, the simple *measurement*

might be the percentage of change over time in the number of participants under 18.

Here's another example. Consider the goal of "More affordable housing." The baseline might be the number of rental units in a certain price range. An indicator of change might be an increase in the number of rental units or perhaps a new range of rental prices. The measurement, then, would be counting the numbers of rental units after a certain period of time and reporting the change, if any.

Who will collect the data? For how long? These are the areas where details are important to making the measurement accurate and useful. Once again, members of a community group can be involved in selecting the goal, the indicator and collecting data for the measurement.

Measuring for success can be a very powerful tool in gaining support for a community activity. Using this type of information to describe results offers excellent marketing and visibility opportunities in local media outlets. A headline that reads, "15% Increase in Affordable Housing" is more significant than one that just says, "Community Project Works on Rental Units."

Community Builder Strategies and Techniques

1. Get Used to It

Make everyone in the group familiar with the experience of evaluation and feedback by ending every single meeting with a very brief conversation about a) what went well b) what didn't go well and c) how we can improve.

2. Make Sure You Learn From Everything

If you're going to try the midpoint correction concept, follow through and respond to feedback with action. If people complain about long meetings, make sure the meetings get shorter! If you get data that says a certain strategy didn't work, don't keep using it.

3. Try a Subcommittee

Recruit or let three people self-select for an oversight committee to manage ongoing evaluation. Let them handle the end of the meeting discussion, design a one-page evaluation form for the town hall meeting or hold a focus group on the project.

4. Focus on Just a Few Items

No group should be overwhelmed by a list of goals so long that there will never be an end in sight. Try selecting just a few items for evaluation or progress checks rather than trying to be so global that the information is diffused and useless.

5. Be Creative and Try Unobtrusive Evaluations

This is an approach that gathers feedback while nobody notices. For example, if you have an exhibit in town and you want to see which piece is most popular, check out the carpet wear and tear. Worn areas will tell you where people stay the longest. Another example is allowing participants to self-select for discussion topics. If nobody goes to the table to talk about repaving main street, it might not really be an issue.

Troubleshooting

Nobody Cares!

Trying to get a feedback loop on progress installed in a project can bring the community builder right up against a seeming lack of interest. It's also not unusual for a community project to be the last topic a local newspaper wants to feature or only of interest to the folks involved first hand.

- Watch your timing. Maybe the point at which attendance has dropped off isn't the right time to form an evaluation committee. Try this when energy is high.
- Use photographs and local names when you report progress to the newspaper. This rarely fails to get the attention of the local press.
- Delegate participants to carry the word about progress. Craft a message together and ask for each member to tell 10 other folks (even relatives count in a small town!).
- Facilitate a focus group. Invite six or seven non-members to coffee and talk about the project. Ask them for some feed-back on visibility and support of the project. Then report to the group.
- Get on agendas. Offer reports to officials at council and commission meetings and also to service clubs. If you can find some high school kids to work together to do a 10-minute report, you'll find that everyone will listen.

We're Too Busy To Stop and Think

Really questioning if any progress is being made takes some time to reflect. Few people have the luxury of taking time in that way, and few groups regularly have retreats or planning sessions that involve any quiet time. The issue is how to get folks to slow down once the action starts, in order to see if any changes might be helpful.

- Focus questions are helpful. In a meeting session, it often works just to ask a question such as, "What part of our project is working the best right now?" and give everyone five minutes of silent time to thing about it before sharing.

- Try a retreat. Spending a half day together in a different setting can get some reflection and review going.
- Pair up for evaluation. In a meeting session, use pairs or trios to develop some evaluation questions.
- Some people like homework. Ask everyone to think about improvement ideas and either email or postal mail them to you. Start the next meeting with the responses.
- Invite a guest speaker to talk about a project in terms of what was learned.

If It's Not Broken— Well, You Know the Rest

Change and improvement is tough to sell, especially with long-standing events. The role of a community event might change over time but the program and the volunteer committee might stay the same. Over time, procedures can become sacred traditions and create a real resistance to change.

- Sometimes the first answer isn't the best answer. Use brainstorming to generate lots of alternatives and help the group to think creatively.

- Get more kids involved. Adults usually know what NOT to ask, but sometimes a younger member can suggest new ideas and be accepted.
- Use comparisons. This is where the visit to another town or description of a similar event can make innovation more palatable to the tradition defenders.
- Set some new goals or revisit the purpose. Why be satisfied with goals that were developed years ago? Events and projects can have more than one impact, so this is a way to review and make the most of an ongoing activity.
- Play "What if...?" Generate some alternative scenarios and discuss the idea in terms of consequences, not costs or degree of change.

From the Field

The Scenario

The community actually encompasses the three-county area of Bent, Crowley and Otero Counties. The situation that needed to be addressed initially was a declining stock of satisfactory housing. In the early 1980s, a housing rehabilitation program had been serving the area. Plagued with compliance and administrative concerns, the program was shut down. However, the housing situation did not go away. Few houses or apartment facilities were being constructed, and there were few gaps in the available housing market. In 1991, the town of Fowler, Colorado, initiated plans to reconstitute the housing rehabilitation program. The

result of this initiative was Tri-County Housing, Inc.

Tools or Techniques Used to Respond to the Issue

The initial focus was on developing a core group of entities. These pioneers were actually municipalities and counties that supported the program financially, as well as appointing representatives to serve on the organization's board of directors. This involvement provided instant credibility for the program. In essence, it mended any fences that were a residual negative of the previous program. The original budget for the housing rehabilitation program was approximately $300,000, and had a staff of one. Today, that budget figure is $1.345 million and has a staff of eight. While housing rehab remains as the basis of the agency's program, it has expanded into self-help construction, property management, community development, multi-family developments, and other programs.

The initial challenge was to stay above water. This required a commitment to do the simple things

well...to have measurable successes, i.e., 10 houses rehabilitated, or a loan portfolio of $200,000. This small steps to success approach worked extremely well. The participating entities became stronger supporters of the organization, and various funding sources became more available. The board members allowed each other the opportunity to grow, not only as individuals, but also as a team. In addition, the members treated each other with respect—everyone had a voice.

The old adage that success breeds success held true. The board of directors became more willing to take calculated risks. New ventures became learning experiences and innovative approaches to solving the housing situation. Tri-County Housing was chosen as one of the original members of the Rural LISC family, and recently received word that it has been approved as a new start in the NeighborWorks network. Both affiliations offer numerous opportunities for training, capacity building, financing, fundraising and networking. The capacity building opportunities provided by Rural LISC have included funding, technical assistance, and organizational planning. Staff and board members have also taken advantage of training provided through the NeighborWorks program. These skills will in turn help the participating entities formulate their own paths to success. Success breeds success.

Lessons Learned from the Development Experience

Dynamic leadership is an essential element of any successful organization. You must allow this leadership to grow, because that growth will enable you to trust and communicate in an open manner. Each member of the board or your committee is an important resource. Their opinions and ideas are an integral part of your organization's mission, character and philosophy. Park your ego and your political party at the door.

One of the keys to Tri-County's success was its board. It came to an early conclusion that the success of its program delivery and impact would be because it would have to do it. There were no other agencies, municipal or otherwise, that could step in and fill the void. The dynamics and relationships that are developed within an organization are critical. Always keep an eye on your mission and your philosophical vision.

A commitment to excellence was established early...whether consciously or due to survival. You can look to the future, but you have to take care of the present. Even though Tri-County has expanded its programmatic functions, the housing rehabilitation program continues to be an integral part of the organization.

Be conscious of your audience. If you don't toot your own horn, nobody else will. Media relations are an extremely important asset that only a select few access—you have to get the word out. Sell your success and your viewing public's opportunities.

Sometimes you have to take a chance. However, if you have the framework in place, then the chance of failure can be minimized.

Commitment to your mission. Even though you might get sidetracked, stay focused. Your consistency and adherence to that philosophy results in a buy-in by the staff, the board, your funding resources, and the general public.

— *Barry Shioshita*
Colorado

Chapter Seven
Coaching: Linking Knowledge to Action in the 21st Century

At one time, the word coach conjured up a football field or tennis court. Often today, however, we hear people talking about coaching people, organizations, businesses, employees, and groups. In fact, the term has taken on new meaning; some say it's become an organizational development fad.

If we define coaching as a process of helping people, organizations, and groups think and work better together, we can see many uses for coaching in the realm of community building. In fact, many community builders have honed key coaching skills in the work they do everyday with communities. You probably have some experience with the help groups need to learn and grow, or ways to use reflection and evaluation when you sought or gave support and suggestions to your colleagues. That can, in fact, be termed coaching.

What makes coaching different from other forms of technical assistance? The very best coaching does not give people answers or solutions, but rather leads them to a new perspective or view of the situation that offers them previously unknown options. Equally important, good coaches help people and groups reflect on what they already know as well as learn from their own experience.

Why Bother?

Is there substance here for community builders? Should coaching become part of the community builder's toolkit? Our answer is emphatically, Yes!

Providing technical assistance and training to communities in the 21st century is dramatically different from previous decades and poses new challenges. Today, everyone can find expertise easily by accessing the Internet. Because this information is so easily available, we are rethinking both the *value* of expertise and the *delivery* of expertise.

How do we *value* expertise? Our work in community and economic development makes it clear that solutions to community problems are place- or community-based rather than expertise-based. We've all faced the situation when the expert from out of town has no clue about what works and doesn't work in our community. These outside experts with the one right answer often can't deliver on the one right solution we need! The solution must come from within the community. Expertise is useful and we can learn from experts on the web, in books, or in person, but these lessons offer insight rather than perfect answers. The communities we work with must craft their own answers. Thus, expertise in and of itself, is less valuable today if it is not connected to making the expertise work.

Coaches help people connect the right expertise to the right situation. By asking insightful questions they assist communities and groups in shifting through the great pile of data and information to key in on

what is useful. Coaches can even act as mentors to outsiders with the desired expertise to help them relate to the current situation, context and learning needs of those involved.

Coaches Wear Many Different Hats

Coaching is a complex process; it is something we almost all do daily, yet the description and philosophy can be elusive. More and more often we hear of examples of how coaching is making a difference in community settings. In some of the literature, the coach is the outsider who facilitates internal processes or coaches personal growth opportunities. In other examples, the coach is the leader or boss who uses coaching as an effective leadership tool for creating teams, setting and achieving shared goals, and nourishing innovation. In community building the coach is more the guide on the side, a person not directly involved in the process, but one who has a commitment to its success. From the observer's point of view, the coach helps teams work through issues, monitors processes, and offers encouragement. According to Ken Hubbell, former Rural Community College Initiative coach,

Coaching is about the way we walk beside one another for support when things are difficult, for encouragement when we are overwhelmed, and for nurturing our opportunities to learn and share the wisdom of that learning with others.

While coaching involves some teaching, coaches are not teachers who give lessons and test recall. Coaches work to establish co-learning and co-teaching relationships with others to explore how new knowledge and expertise can help groups and communities work toward their vision. Coaches play a role as a consultant; they bring in the outside perspective and provide a fresh look at things, yet coaches do not retain a high level of detachment from the situation; they are in for the long haul. Our successes are their successes; our failures, their concern. Coaching is essentially a reflective activity providing opportunities for others to learn from reflection and integrating reflective work into our everyday lives.

Coaching and Community Building

Good coaches listen well and ask good questions. They are respectful of others and attentive to their own processes. Hargrove[1] sees coaches as people who are vision builders and value shapers. They focus on the future, not the past. Coaching involves a sort of stewardship or a focus on working for a positive future for the community served. Coaches should be attuned to opportunities to empower personal transformation and reinvention to create that future. Coaches assist in facilitating commitment and team collaboration. Finally, coaches work hard to expand people's capacity to take effective action and make for themselves that future.

Communities and groups find coaching assistance particularly helpful in the following areas:

- Assessment: Coaches ask questions and suggest strategies to help groups and individuals assess their strengths and weakness as well as the opportunities or threats in the situation. Coaches search for a way to understand how groups and organizations understand their situation and use that understanding to lead them to new

---

1 Hargrove, Robert. *Masterful Coaching: Extraordinary Results by Impacting People and the Way They Think and Work Together.* Josey Bass, 1995.

ways of seeing and thinking, and thus new ways of doing.

- Strategizing: Coaches help people and groups determine what strategies will help them make a difference by analyzing the information to find the opening or teachable moment and working to find a way to make a connection on a meaningful level, creating the *ah ha* moment.

- Gaining commitment: Coaches help people and groups make a commitment to move forward, set urgent compelling, stretch goals and achieve a first success.

- Making things happen: By helping people and groups develop new skills and perspectives, and alter or expand their way of looking at a problem, coaches help people and groups find their way to actionable steps and pay attention to timelines and accountability issues.

- Reflection: Coaches help people take the learning and understanding they get from their work to the next level by continually reflecting on what works and what doesn't, adding new knowledge and perspectives, and creating opportunities to see and do things differently.

Coaching is not a simple linear activity, but rather a complex cycle of interactions that feed back upon one another. Coaching, as an approach to community work, also offers a unique opportunity for personal and professional development.

Pay Attention to Strategies and Techniques

1. Good Coaching Is Intentional Coaching

Successful coaching is intentional rather than accidental, meaning that coaching requires us to consciously step out of other roles to take on the mantle of coach. As coach we listen more than we speak; we ask probing questions gracefully. In this role, we don't give answers, we throw requests for opinion back to the group. We listen hard to grasp the underlying rationale behind the group's thinking, and we help make explicit the link or lack of links between facts, analysis, opinion and judgment.

2. Coaching Requires a Degree of Detachment

As coaches, we want to think carefully about the questions: What is my role here? What does the group need me to focus on? What does the group need to better understand about its own process and situation? How is the group working? As we work with the group, we want to think of ourselves as outside the group where we can observe both the group's work and our role. Effective coaching requires us to detach from our own agenda and interests and focus attention completely on what the group is doing.

3. Coaching Is Essentially a Reflective Activity

Effective coaches are perpetually in the learning mode. Every coaching event is an opportunity to learn more about ourselves and our work. Effective coaches build in reflection time by keeping journals, working with mentors, and/or developing supportive networks among fellow community builders.

4. Facilitating Relationships With Coaching

Successful coaching requires a willingness on the part of all involved to engage in ongoing learning and to try new things. Coaching is a two-way street. Without agreement to participate, coaching devolves into teaching, lecturing or cajoling. It would be better to back out and wait for another time. Everyone involved must also be sensitive to the personal nature of coaching. Coaches that put the difficult issues on the table can help people acknowledge where the sore spots are likely to be, so they can be dealt with.

5. Coaching Depends on Trust

Coaches who make a difference in groups do so because the group trusts the coach to act in their best interest. Trust is something that must be nurtured and protected. Coaches can build trust by keeping group business within the group, by acknowledging what they don't know, and by trusting the group.

6. Coaches as Cheerleaders

One of the most useful roles coaches play in groups is to remind them of successes and strengths. Coaches call attention to the achievement of mileposts. They acknowledge the wisdom of the group, and they recognize the contributions of group members.

7. Skills Associated with Coaching

Master coaches often have an aura of mystique and mastery around them such that some people feel that coaching is a function of personality. Because we believe that coaching is a skill that people can

learn and practice, we have included this chapter on what coaching is and how it works, as well as suggesting opportunities for practicing coaching skills. The skills set associated with coaching include basic skills from the following areas:

- Communications
- Feedback
- Reflection
- Facilitation
- Adult Learning

One way to practice coaching is to identify a situation where you see yourself as having a coaching function. Set carefully thought out coaching goals for that situation and identify the skills you think you will need to put in use. Many of us like to put these thoughts on paper and use the results as a sort of worksheet to keep notes as we work through the situation. After the coaching session is over, use your preparation and work notes to reflect on what worked, what didn't work, what might have been an alternative approach, what you learned about the group and yourself, and what skills you want to practice next.

Troubleshooting

Getting Your Group Out of a Rut

How often have you been to a meeting where everyone has all the reasons why things won't work, why the community won't change, or why nobody really cares? Most interventions end up as an invitation to an even gloomier round of reasons why. Groups like these are stuck dead center in a rut of negativity. Every potential solution leads back to the refrain of nobody cares or we tried that before or…. These discussions loop back to the starting point and always end with everyone firmly fixed in the rut. These circumstances often require some sort of coaching to break free.

- *Look for ways to reframe the situation—we can't get anything done because nothing gets done to a different picture.* You could, for example, reframe this conversation by discussing the normal curve of adopting new practices or adapting to new conditions. You can mention that the willingness to adopt change is, like other human characteristics such as height and weight, char-

acteristic of people that fit on a normal curve: very few short people are at the extreme end of the curve; very few tall people are at the other extreme end of the curve. Some short people; some tall people toward the ends of curves, and most of us in the middle. Similarly, the curve tells us at the extreme ends we have the innovators who always want to do something new and those who will never change. Next in the curve, on one end we have early adopters who will take advantage of a good idea when they see it, and, on the other end, those who will change kicking and screaming along the way. In the middle are those of us who go along with change once it has a proven record.

- *Help the group change their mental picture of the situation.* When groups are caught in the rut of negativity because they can't see how something can be accomplished, they often have a mental picture of the people at the extreme end of the curve on the

ty or group improve with lots of enthusiastic discussion and idea generation that goes no where. Coaches can help by:

- *Observing and understanding group behavior.* For example, a coach listening to a group talk about all the good reasons to do something might interject a comment to the effect that we seem to all be agreed on the need to do something. This comment will test the appearance of consensus, and if consensus exists, focus attention on what needs to happen next.

"won't-ever-change-no-how" end.

- *Craft an "ah ha" or teachable moment.* What happens to the possibilities for action, when we concentrate on the people at the innovator, early adopter end of the curve? Often this new way of looking at the problem can result in a dramatic *ah ha* moment. Groups can immediately see doable actions when they focus on the right group.

- *Assisting others in setting compelling goals.* Coaches can help the group move from general discussion to what needs to happen to make changes or implement good ideas by asking questions such as, What has to happen first to move forward?

Moving from Discussion to Action

Many groups and communities are pegged with a no-go label. Well-intentioned people struggle to find effective ways to help their communi-

Attending to Cultural Competency

The coach's role as an outsider provides a useful vantage point from which to observe and provide feedback on issues related to diversity and cultural competency by:

- *Helping the group listen to one another.* Coaches can remind the group of suggestions when those ideas get lost in the general discussion.

- *Transforming unproductive discussion to generate collaborative conversations.* Coaches can restate the minority opinion when it is overlooked or ask the group how to respond to different perspectives or problems that emerge from different contexts.
- *Facilitating active participation.* Coaches can empower missing voices by asking for input from those who are often not heard.
- *Reflecting group behavior.* Coaches may also reflect back to the group observations on how they see the group reacting to new and/or different voices.
- *Reminding the group of the minority position.* Sometimes a minority position is stated that does not click with accepted dogma. Coaches can remind the group of those statements and the group's desire to take minority voices seriously. Sometimes the group needs to be reminded several times, which provides an opportunity to help them think about how they hear these voices, but may not listen or attend to them, and to identify ways to

improve their group practice.

Fostering Inclusiveness

Often the major players in communities and groups can get very enthusiastic about projects and programs and mistake silence for agreement. Coaches can help address the need to understand the true meaning of that silence by

- *Asking who is missing.* Coaches can ask questions about what groups or individuals might be impacted by the project and program and how they are represented in the process.
- *Providing alternatives to group think.* Coaches can suggest group decision making and discussion strategies that allow the silent ones opportunity to participate in a non-threatening manner such as small group work, nominal decision making, or paper ballots.
- *Encouraging participation.* Some of the best coaching occurs outside the meeting where coaches can support participation by reinforcing the value of participants' ideas and suggestions, empowering people to engage in group conversations, and giving constructive feedback.

From the Field

The Scenario

Upon experiencing the loss of their major private employer when the Boise Cascade sawmill closed in 1995, the community of Council, Idaho began the process of becoming more proactive in managing change. A variety of technical assistance providers were assembled to assist the community with strategic planning, project planning, grant-writing/fundraising, project design and grant management. These initial efforts have been relatively successful. At a time when the community faced unprecedented economic downturn, an unprecedented number of community-based projects have been accomplished—including the beginning of true economic diversification.

Prioritized community projects such as a new county courthouse and jail, senior citizens' center, city park, and a telecommunications-enhanced small business park have all been realized since the sawmill closed. As these projects moved forward, it became increasingly important for technical assistance providers to act as community men-

tors. In essence, through the planning process, community members had been saying that they needed to become more self-reliant and less dependent upon outside resources. In order to achieve this, the capacity of the human assets in Council needed to be increased along with simply increasing the number of projects. Although good effort has been made to date, this is an area that lags behind the project development activities. The process is still unfolding one day at a time.

Tools and Techniques Used to Respond to the Issue

- Town hall style meetings are held using participatory decision making to develop recovery strategies. (These meetings provided a strong and lasting foundation for helping Council stay on track.)
- A team of consulting community mentors was established to provide immediate technical assistance combined with teaching/capacity building aspects and long-term commitment to the community. (Team mentoring worked well, but with vary-

ing degrees of success. Finding financial support and/or enough volunteer consulting time was difficult.)

- Capacity building training for community volunteers was funded through the W.K. Kellogg Foundation Initiative Managing Information with Rural America. (The program provided a great opportunity for training, with good examples of lasting success—but it was not sustained enough to create widespread integration of the training into everyday practice.)
- Relentless pursuit of existing (and sometimes non-existent) funding programs, financial contributors, non-financial support, and anything remotely connected to support in order to keep efforts moving forward. (These efforts met with good success, and produced creative solutions.)

Lessons Learned from the Development Experience

- There are strong parallels between facilitating systemic community change and the theories/practices of facilitating individual change in the human

behavioral management profession.

- As community and economic development professionals, we have an ethical obligation to become involved with a community for very long periods of time, if necessary—even if financial remuneration is not always available.
- When attempting to instill within a community inclusive practices such as participatory decision making and investing in social (human) capital, there will be a constant tendency to revert to compartmentalized, project specific, and territorial thinking.
- No one really likes to do the hard work of facilitating systemic community change.
- If you do the hard work, systemic community change is inevitable.

— *Jim Birdsall*
Idaho

Bibliography

Appreciative Inquiry

Barrett, Frank J. 1995. Creating Appreciative Learning Cultures. *Organizational Dynamics*. V. 24, No.2, p. 36.

Cooperrider, David L. 1996. Resources for Getting Appreciative Inquiry Started: An Example OD Proposal. *OD Practitioner*, V.28, No.1-2, p. 23.

Cooperrider, David L. and Diana Whitney. 1999. *Appreciative Inquiry*. San Francisco: Berrett-Koehler Communications, Inc.

Hammond, Sue Annis. 1996. *The Thin Book of Appreciative Inquiry*. Plano, Texas: Thin Book Publishing Company.

Srivastva, Suresh, and David L. Cooperrider. (Eds.) 1990. *Appreciative Management and Leadership*. San Francisco: Jossey-Bass. Reissued by Williams Custom Publishing, available through www.thinbook.com.

Citizen Participation

Franzich, Stephen. *Citizen Democracy*. 1999. Totowa, New Jersey: Rowan and Littlefield.

Hinsdale, Mary Ann, Helen Lewis, and Maxine Waller. *It Comes From the People*. 1995. Philadelphia: Temple University Press.

Johnson, Allan. *Privilege, Power and Difference*. 2001. New York: McGraw Hill.

Loeb, Paul Rogat. *Soul of a Citizen*. 1999. New York: St. Martins Press.

Putnam, Robert D. 1993. *Making Democracy Work: Civic Traditions in Modern Italy*. Princeton, NJ: Princeton University Press.

Wheatley, Margaret. 2002. *Turning to One Another: Simple Conversations to Restore Hope to the Future*. San Francisco: Berrett-Koehler.

Collaboration

Chrislip, David, and Carl Larson. *Collaborative Leadership: How Citizens and Civic Leaders Can Make a Difference*. 1994. San Francisco: Jossey-Bass.

Mattessich, Paul and Mart Murray-Close. 2001. *Collaboration: What Makes It Work*. St. Paul, Minnesota: Amherst H. Wilder Foundation.

Winer, Michael and Karen Ray. 1994. *Collaboration Handbook: Creating, Sustaining, and Enjoying the Journey*. St. Paul, Minnesota: Amherst H. Wilder Foundation.

Communities & Development

Grisham, Vaughn L. 1999. *Tupelo: The Evolution of a Community*. Dayton, Ohio: Kettering Foundation Press.

Grisham, Vaughn and Rob Gurwitt. 1999. *Hand In Hand: Community and Economic Development in Tupelo*. Washington, DC: Aspen Institute Publications. http://www.aspeninst.org/; 410-827-9174.

Hammond, Sue Annis, and Cathy Royal, editors.1998. *Lessons from the Field*. Plano, Texas: Practical Press Inc.

Kinsley, Michael J. 1997. *Economic Renewal Guide: A Collaborative Process for Sustainable Community Development*. Snowmass, Colorado: Rocky Mountain Institute.

Jones, Ellis. 2001. *The Better World Handbook: From Good Intentions to Everyday Actions*. Gabriola Island, B.C., Canada: New Society Publishers www.betterworldhandbook.com

Kemmis, Dan. *Community and the Politics of Place*. 1992. Norman, Oklahoma: University of Okalahoma Press.

Kretzmann, John P. and John L. McKnight. 1993. *Building Communities from the Inside Out*. Chicago: Northwestern University Press.

Luther, Vicki and Milan Wall. *Clues to Rural Community Survival*. 1998. Lincoln, Nebraska: Heartland Center for Leadership Development.

Luther, Vicki and Milan Wall. *The Entrepreneurial Community: A Strategic Leadership Approach to Community Survival.* 2002. Lincoln, Nebraska: Heartland Center for Leadership Development.

Mattessich, Paul and Barbara Monsey. *Community Building: What Makes It Work.* 1997. St. Paul, Minnesota: Amherst H. Wilder Foundation.

Putnam, Robert. 1995. *Bowling Alone.* New York: Simon and Schuster.

Schaeffer, Peter V. and Scott Loveridge, editors. *Small Town and Rural Economic Development: A Case Studies Approach.* 2000. Westport, Connecticut: Praeger.

Senge, P. 1990. *The Fifth Discipline.* New York: Doubleday.

Shaffer, Carolyn, Kristin Anendsen, M. Scott Peck. 1993. *Finding Community Anywhere.* New York: Perigee Press.

Shuman, Michael H. 1998. *Going Local: Creating Self-reliant Communities in a Global Age.* New York: The Free Press.

Snow, Luther K. 2001. *The Organization of Hope: A Workbook for Rural Asset-Based Community Development.* Chicago: ACTA Publications.

Tropman, John. *Successful Community Leadership.* 1997. Washington, DC: National Association of Social Workers.

Conflict Management

Borisoff, Deborah and David A. Victor. 1997. *Conflict Management: A Communication Skills Approach*. Boston: Allyn & Bacon.

Goldsmith, Joan, and Kenneth Cloke. 2000. *Resolving Conflicts at Work*. San Francisco: Jossey-Bass.

Pachter, Barbara, and Susan McGee. 2001. *Power of Positive Confrontation*. New York: Marlowe and Co.

Facilitation

Craven, Robin, 2001. *Complete Idiots' Guide to Meeting and Event Planning*. Indianapolis, Indiana: Alpha Books.

Doyle, Michael, David Strauss, 1993. *How to Make Meetings Work*. New York: Berkley Publishing

Frank, Milo O., 1989. *How to Run a Successful Meeting in Half the Time*. New York: Simon and Schuster.

Haynes, Marion E. 1997. *Effective Meeting Skills*. Menlo Park, California: Crisp Publications.

Pike, Bob and Dave Arch. 1997. *Dealing With Difficult Participants*. San Francisco: Jossey-Bass/Pfeiffer.

Simon, Judith Sharken. 1999. *The Wilder Nonprofit Field Guide to Conducting Successful Focus Groups*. St. Paul, Minnesota: Amherst H. Wilder Foundation.

Fundraising

Keegan, P. Burke. 1990. *Fundraising for Non-Profits*. New York: Harper Collins Publishers.

Rosso, Henry A. 1991. *Achieving Excellence in Fundraising*. San Francisco: Jossey-Bass.

Group Process

Corey, Marianne Schneider and Gerald Corey. 2001. *Groups: Process and Practice*. Stamford, Connecticut: Wadsworth Publishing Company.

Ephross, Paul and Thomas Vassil. 1988. *Groups That Work: Structure and Process*. New York: Columbia University Press.

Hunter, Dale, Anne Bailey and Bill Taylor. 1995. *The Zen of Groups: A Handbook for People Meeting with a Purpose*. Cambridge, Massachusetts: Fisher Books.

Johnson, David and Frank Johnson. 1999. *Joining Together: Group Theory and Group Skills*. (7th edition). Boston: Allyn & Bacon.

Leadership

De Pree, Max. 1997. *Leading Without Power: Finding Hope in Serving Community*. 1997. San Francisco: Jossey-Bass.

Heifetz, Ron. 1994. *Leadership Without Easy Answers*. Harvard University: Belknap Press.

Luke, Jeffrey S. 1998. *Catalytic Leadership*. San Francisco, CA: Jossey-Bass Publishers.

Wall, Milan and Vicki Luther. 2001. *Building Local Leadership: How to Start a Program for Your Town or County*. Lincoln, Nebraska: Heartland Center for Leadership Development.

Tropman, John. 1997. *Successful Community Leadership*. Washington, DC: National Association of Social Workers.

Wheatley, Margaret J. 1992. *Leadership and the New Science: Learning about Organization from an Orderly Universe*. San Francisco: Berrett-Koehler.

Wheatley, Margaret. 2001. Restoring Hope to the Future Through Critical Education of Leaders. *The Nonprofit Quarterly*. Fall, 2001.

Marketing

Horowitz, Shel. 2002. *Grassroots Marketing: Getting Noticed in a Noisy World*. White River Junction, New Jersey: Chelsea Green Publishing Company.

Bray, Robert. 2002. *Spin Works*. San Francisco: Independent Media Institute.

Stern, Gary J. 1997. *Marketing Workbook for Nonprofit Organizations, Vol.II: Mobilize People for Marketing Success*. St. Paul, Minnesota: Amherst H. Wilder Foundation.

Stern, Gary J. 2001. *Marketing Workbook for Nonprofit Organizations, Vol. I: Develop the Plan, 2nd edition*. St. Paul, Minnesota: Amherst H. Wilder Foundation.

Non-Profit Organizations

Angelica, Emil and Vincent Hyman. 1997. *Coping With Cutbacks: The Nonprofit Guide to Success When Times Are Tight.* St. Paul, Minnesota: Amherst Wilder Foundation.

Angelica, Marion Peters. 1999. *Resolving Conflict in Nonprofit Organizations.* St. Paul, Minnesota: Amherst H. Wilder Foundation.

Austin, James. 2000. *The Collaboration Challenge: How Nonprofits and Businesses Succeed Through Strategic Alliances.* San Francisco: Jossey-Bass.

Bonk, Kathy, Henry Griggs and Emily Tynes. 1999. *Strategic Communications for Nonprofits.* San Francisco: Jossey-Bass.

Cumfer, Cynthia & Kay Sohl. 2001. *The Oregon Non-profit Corporation Handbook.* Portland, Oregon: Technical Assistance for Community Services.

Kiritz, Norton J. 1980. *Program Planning and Proposal Writing.* Los Angeles: The Grantsmanship Center.

Srivastva, Suresh and Ronald Fry (Eds.) 1992. *Executive and Organizational Continuity.* San Francisco: Jossey-Bass.

Skills Development

Argyris, Chris. 1993. *Knowledge for Action.* San Francisco: Jossey-Bass.

Bone, Diane. 1994. *The Business Of Listening.* Menlo Park. California: Crisp Publications, Inc.

Booher, Dianna. 1994. *Communicate with Confidence*. New York: McGraw-Hill.

Condrell, Jo and Bernice Bough. 1999. *101 Ways to Improve Your Communication Skills Instantly*. Los Angeles: GoalMinds.

Covey, Stephen. 1990. *Seven Habits of Highly Effective People*. New York: Simon and Schuster.

Eisaguirre, Lynne. 2002. *The Power of a Good Fight*. Indianapolis, Indiana: Alpha Books.

Ellis, Keith. 1998. *The Magic Lantern: Goal Setting for People Who Hate Goal Setting*. Three Rivers, Michigan: Three Rivers Press.

Fanning, Patrick, Matthew McKay and Martha Davis. 1995. *Messages: The Communication Skills Book*. Oakland, California: New Harbringer Publishing.

Fisher, Roger and Scott Brown. 1989. *Getting Together: Building Relationships As We Negotiate*. USA: Penguin.

Kotter, John. *Leading Change*. 1996. Cambridge, Massachusetts: Harvard Business School Press.

Lao Tzu, *Tao Te Ching*. The Tao Te Ching is an ancient Chinese book of wisdom, rich in insights on the nature of leadership. There are many translations available.

Kusuya, Beverly. 1997. *Speak Up: Conversations and Cross Cultural Communication*. Baltimore, Maryland: Addison-Wesley.

Miller, Marlene. 1997. *Brain Styles: Change your Life without Changing Who You Are.* New York: Simon & Schuster.

Smith, Douglas. 1999. *Make Success Measurable: A Mindbook-Workbook for Setting Goals and Taking Action.* New York: John Wiley & Sons.

Wilder, Claudyne and David Fine. 1996. *Point, Click & Wow!! A Guide to Brilliant Laptop Presentations.* San Diego, California: Pfeiffer & Company.

Williams, Mark, Donald Clifton. 2001. *The 10 Lenses: Living and Working in a Multicultural World.* Herndon, Virginia: Capital Books.

Williamson, Bruce. 1993. *Playful Activities for Powerful Presentations.* Duluth, Minnesota: Whole Person Associates Inc.

Stone, Douglas, Sheila Heed and Roger Fisher. 1999. *Difficult Conversations: How to Discuss What Matters Most.* New York: Bantam Books. (Compact Disc).

Social Capital

Coleman, James. 1988. Social Capital in the Creation of Human Capital. *American Journal of Sociology.* 94:S95-S120.

Granovetter, Mark S., 1973. The Strength of Weak Ties. *The Journal of American Sociology* (Vol. 78, Issue 6, May, 1973). http://social.capital.unl.edu/

Strategic Planning

Gable, Cate. 1999. *Strategic Action Planning Now: A Guide for Setting and Meeting Your Goals.* Boca Raton, Florida: CRC Press.

Audio Cassettes

Lee, Blaine. 1998. The Power Principle: Influencing with Honor. New York: Fireside Press.

Videos

Dealing with Differences and Difficult People. 65 minutes. Advantage Coaching and Training. Wheaton, Illinois. www.advantagecoaching.com

Klein, Kim. Grassroots Fundraising Training Videos. *#1 Planning For Fundraising, #4 Asking for Money and Prospect Identification. #6 Special Events.* Funded by the Youth Project. Washington D.C. 2334 18th St. 20009. 202-483-0030.

Meetings Bloody Meetings. John Cleese. 1978. Video Arts Group. London. UK. (30 minutes) A veteran of Monte Python's Flying Circus takes on the topic of meetings. sales@lettucetrainu.com

Web Sites

For project ideas:
National Main Street Program http://www.mainst.org/awards

For Appreciative Inquiry:
Appreciative Inquiry Commons
http://www.Appreciativeinquiry.cwru.edu
Pew Partnership for Civic Change www.pew-partnership.org
Marlene Coroselli, Ed.D. http://hometown.aol.com/mccpd

Communities by Choice:
http://www.communitiesbychoice.org/

A compendium of how to instructions from time management to making a plan:
http://4h.unl.edu/volun/arlen/atoolkit.htm.

Many articles and books on social capital in families, communities, and civic society:
http://www.worldbank.org/poverty/scapital/

Good definitions, exceptions to social capital and critique from the British perspective:
http://www.statistics.gov.uk/themes/social-finances/socialcapital.asp

International Association of Facilitators:
www.iaf-world.org

The Meeting Wizard website offers tips on effective meetings and online tools for meeting planning:
http://www.meetingwizard.org/

iVisit.com offers free software, online help and meeting space to experiment with online meetings:
http://www.ivisit.com/

Alliance of National Renewal:
http://www.policity.com/

Books on grassroots fundraising plus articles from back issues of the Grassroots Fundraising Journal:
http://www.grassrootsfundraising.org/index.html.

National organization with references on various community and economic development topics:
http://www.communitychange.org/default.asp.

The Grantsmanship Center. A great resource on foundations and grant writing:
http://www.tgci.com

Valdis Kreb's organization, OrgNet, has extensive resources for mapping personal and organizational networks:
http://www.orgnet.com/

The New Community Collaboration Manual. 1991. *This may be ordered from the National Assembly of National Voluntary Health and Social Welfare Organizations:*
http://www.nassembly.org/

Wilder Foundation's Collaboration Factors Inventory: This inventory provides a way for potential partners or existing collaborations to see how they rate themselves on key factors for successful collaboration. The inventory may be taken online or ordered from their website:
http://www.wilder.org/pubs/inventory/CollaborationA.html

A good summary of lobbying tips:
http://www.calvoter.org/legguide/lobbyingtips.html

*The following are websites related to accessing
information/articles on Congress:*
http://www.citizen.org/index.cfm
http://www.thecapitol.net

League of Women Voters:
http://www.lwv.org

*Developed by Campaign Consultation, Inc., this site has
several useful pages including tools and library materials
that can be downloaded. Try the page below for a marketing
plan template:*
http://www.sustainabilityonline.com
http://www.sustainabilityonline.com/html/Articles/Gettingthew
or.pdf

*This site offers free tips on co-marketing with other groups,
finding corporate sponsors in depressed areas, writing feature
stories, creating surveys and storytelling for grant seekers:*
http://www.nonprofitmarketing.org
or www.gb3group.com

*Brushy Fork Institute of Berea College
Since 1988, Brushy Fork Institute has worked to develop
strong leadership in Appalachian communities throughout
Kentucky, Tennessee, Virginia and West Virginia:*
http://www.berea.edu/brushyfork

Extra Resources and Activities from the Heartland Center

Please use, adapt and improve!
Just be sure to give the Heartland Center credit
if you copy the following items.

Five Never Fail Get-Acquainted Activities

1. Tonight's Question Is…

The discussion leader develops a question related to the work topic then directs the participants to answer the question, then stand up, find a partner and share. After five to ten minutes, the group leader reconvenes the group and samples three or four answers. This provides the transition into the meeting content.

2. What's the History of Your Name

The group leader uses some method to form pairs then directs each person to share the history of her/his name with their partner. Responses can be sampled or used to introduce each partner to the entire group.

3. Tell Us Your Name and One More Item

Select an item that will help move to the content of the session. For example, "Tell us what you like best about your town".

4. Think of a…

In this activity, the leader selects a category of an ideal role model appropriate to the group and the topic. For example,

"Think of the best communicator you ever heard" or "Think of the best community celebration you ever attended". Responses can be shared at tables or listed person by person to then move into the work topic.

5. Find Someone Who...

Using a list developed prior to the session, each participant is asked to talk with other individuals to locate skills, experiences and interests in the group. Work-related items can be alternated with fun topics. For example, Find Someone Who...has written a successful grant followed by Find Someone Who... knows a great zucchini bread recipe.

Town Hall Sampler

Promotion

•

Roles

•

Agenda

•

Discussion Guide

•

Evaluation Form

Promoting a Town Hall Meeting

Make sure you promote the meeting throughout the community through a variety of methods. Here is a list to get you started:

- Special invitations to people in recognized leadership positions such as officers of service clubs, church organizations, chambers of commerce, elected and appointed officials, ministers.
- Press release or notice for newspapers, radios and any organizational newsletter that your community members might receive.
- Notices, posters, flyers in well-traveled places in the community.
- Use of "telephone trees" within service clubs and other organizations to invite community members.
- Sending an invitation to families from the school, notice in the school bulletin or a flyer sent home with students.
- Including an invitation with the monthly water bill.
- Rent a portable, lighted signboard and place it prominently so folks will notice.
- Use e-mail reminders.

Conducting The Town Hall Meeting

Actually, conducting a town hall meeting isn't difficult if you have an active steering committee or group that will divide the tasks into manageable parts. Several roles are particularly important and should be considered carefully by the group.

Greeters

Host/hostess to greet people at the door, thank them for coming and ask them to sign in at the registration table.

Registration Table

Two or more people to manage an area for sign in and hand out materials.

Convener

An individual who will be recognized by most members of the community and who will lend credibility to the meeting, provide the official welcome and introduce the first activity and close the meeting at the end of the evening.

Activity Leader

An individual who has become familiar with the Trends activity and can direct participants to form smaller groups, then provide a summary of the activity at the end of the meeting.

Discussion Leaders

Individuals who can help groups of seven to ten community members work through the Trends Discussion activity and direct participants to small group sessions.

Sample Agenda for a Town Hall Meeting

The following agenda is provided as a sample. It is very flexible and can be adapted to unique needs in each community.

7:00 p.m.   **Registration and Coffee**
Participants get name tag, agenda and evaluation sheet

7:30   **Share agenda**
- Purpose of the meeting
- Introduce activity leader

7:40   **Share project update**
- Importance of future to community
- Value of discussion and citizen participation

7:45   **Trends Activity**
1. Break into small groups
2. Facilitators lead discussion and record ideas: use *Both Sides of the Trend* activity
3. Flip chart sheets posted, large group meets

8:45   **Break and refreshments**
while participants visit and read flip chart sheets

9:00   ***Both Sides of the Trend***
- Begin discussion of future
- If interested, people can work on these threats/ opportunities
- Announce that information recorded on flip chart sheets will be made available to elected and appointed officials

9:15   **Closing and Evaluation**
Participants fill out evaluation sheet

9:30   **Steering Committee meets to read evaluation forms and discuss next steps.**
- What would you have changed about this meeting?
- What specific actions do you see?

Sample Town Hall Activity

Both Sides of the Trend:
A Discussion Guide

This exercise is designed to help groups begin to focus on those trends that are most significant to the future of their community and to identify the threats and opportunities represented by those trends.

The basic design of this activity is a structured discussion in which group members decide on a trend that they wish to discuss and then analyze the impacts of that trend in terms of the threats and opportunities it will bring.

For example, an obvious trend that small towns must deal with is the increasing age of their population. This change in the demographic profile of their citizens may be a threat in some ways (having tremendous impacts on housing and health care needs) but in other ways might prove to be an opportunity (in areas of retired volunteers or business opportunities in services to the elderly).

The guide is based on likely rural trends and outlines this activity step-by-step, from selecting a recorder to keep track of the discussion, to brainstorming guidelines, to samples of group discussion questions. The list of trends can be adapted or updated.

The time required for this activity will vary depending on the amount of time allowed for discussion. However, you should plan on 1 to 1 1/2 hours to complete this discussion activity.

Worksheet for Town Hall Activity

Goals:

1. To structure the discussion of probable trends on the positive and negative impacts of each trend.

2. To help keep the discussion focused on a particular topic.

3. To organize the information and ideas that come from the discussion.

Please read the directions as your group proceeds through the discussion:

1. As a group, select a recorder who will keep track of the discussion on the newsprint provided.

2. As an individual, take a look at the following list of trends and pick one that seems most significant to you.

Trends:

- Likely consolidation of government and business services into larger towns.
- Continuing debate over moral/ethical issues in health care.
- New tax sources necessary to maintain quality education at all levels.
- Decrease in the number of independently owned banks.
- Great expansion of telecommunications and information available by direct access.
- Fewer farms, more regulation of natural resources, and expanded products and processing in agriculture.
- More manufacturing jobs.
- Increased services to the elderly.

Worksheet for Town Hall Activity

3. In turn, each member should tell the group which trend he or she picked as most significant. *(You might want to record the other group members' choices here.)*

4. As a group, select a trend to discuss in depth. *(The recorder should list this choice on newsprint.)*

Worksheet for Town Hall Activity

5. Your task now is to create a list of the threats represented by this trend and the opportunities it may bring.

Trend: _____

Threats	Opportunities

Worksheet for Town Hall Activity

6. Now, as a group, create a list that will include all the ideas that each individual has developed. Your recorder should list these ideas on the flip chart provided. **Make sure that everyone's ideas are included.**

7. When your group has finished creating a list of the threats and opportunities that will result from a probable trend, you might want to take some time to discuss some of the ideas.

   • Can any of the threats be minimized?

   • Can any of the opportunities be maximized?

   • How can communities prepare for the threats of the trend you discussed?

   • How can communities make the most of the opportunities created by this trend.

8. Listen for directions for sharing your work with the total group.

Town Hall Sample Evaluation Form

1. What did you like best about this activity?

2. What did you like the least?

3. The most important thing I learned was...

4. The way this activity was designed and conducted made me feel...

5. How would you rate this activity in achieving its goals?

Goal I: _____

(*Not At All*)   1   2   3   4   5   (*Very Successful*)

Goal II: _____

(*Not At All*)   1   2   3   4   5   (*Very Successful*)

Goal III: _____

(*Not At All*)   1   2   3   4   5   (*Very Successful*)

Fist-to-Five Consensus Process

When a group comes to consensus on a matter, it means that everyone in the group can support the decision; they don't all have to think it's the best decision, but they all agree that they can live with it. Whenever a group is discussing a possible solution or coming to a decision on any matter, Fist-to-Five is a good tool to determine everyone's opinion. To use this technique, the group leader restates a decision under discussion and asks each participant to show his or her level of support. Each person responds by showing a fist or a number of fingers that corresponds to a level of support.

- *Fist:* a "no" vote — block consensus. "I need to talk more about the proposal and require changes for it to pass."

- *1 Finger:* wait a bit — "I still need to discuss certain issues and suggest changes that should be made."

- *2 Fingers:* OK, but — "I'm more comfortable with the decision, but would like to discuss some minor issues."

- *3 Fingers:* OK — "I'm not in total agreement but feel comfortable enough to let this decision pass without further discussion."

- *4 Fingers:* Yes — "I think it's a good decision and will work for it."

- *5 Fingers:* You bet! "It's a great decision, and I'll be one of the leaders in implementing it."

If anyone shows fewer than three fingers, he or she should be given the opportunity to state objections and the team should address these concerns. Groups continue the Fist-to-Five process until they achieve consensus (everyone shows a minimum of three fingers or higher of support).

This activity was developed by the American Youth Foundation. Used with permission.

Community Development Idea Marketplace

This format for sharing ideas can be used as part of any community gathering, meeting or conference. The only requirements for an Idea Marketplace are:

- Copies of the Marketplace Form
- Wall area large enough to display completed forms

Participants complete the form prior to the meeting and the forms are collected as participants arrive.

All the forms are then displayed—at eye level or lower—so that during a coffee break, people can browse and read. A hallway works well. If feasible, copies can be stapled together as a document and distributed.

Idea Marketplace

Information about community projects that really work, new ideas in community economic development, techniques that you've tried or seen used in a community setting are all ideas that can be exchanged as part of the Idea Marketplace.

Please complete this form, describing whatever idea, technique, strategy, concept, project, approach, success, risk, or inspiration you'd like to share. All forms will be collected and displayed as part of the Idea Marketplace.

Name _____

Title _____

Organization_____

Address _____

City _____ State _____ ZIP_____

Phone _____

1. Community Development Idea
   (*Describe your idea in a few words.*)

2. What did you learn or discover as a result of using this idea?

Room Arrangements for Large Gatherings

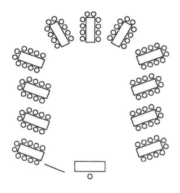

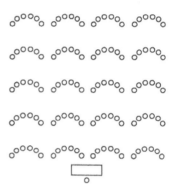

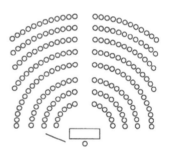

Room Arrangements for Small Work Groups

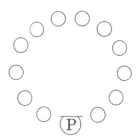

Chairs in a Circle

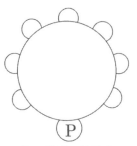

Round Table with Chairs

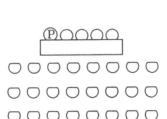

Theater-Style Arrangement
with Chairs

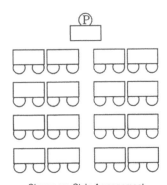

Classroom-Style Arrangement
with Table and Chairs

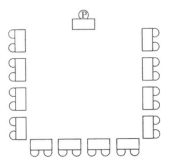

U Shape with Table and Chairs

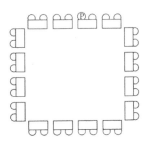

Square/Rectangle with Table and Chairs

Room Arrangements for Small Work Groups

Diamond with Table and Chairs

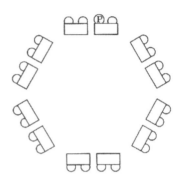

Hexagon with Table and Chairs

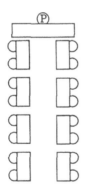

T Shape with Table and Chairs

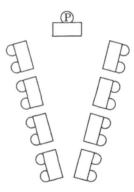

Classroom-Style V Shape
with Table and Chairs

Community Development Society
Principles of Good Practice

- Promote active and representative participation toward enabling all community members to meaningfully influence the decisions that affect their lives.

- Engage community members in learning about and understanding community issues, and the economic, social, environmental, political, psychological, and other impacts associated with alternative courses of action.

- Incorporate the diverse interests and cultures of the community in the community development process; and disengage from support for any effort that is likely to adversely affect the disadvantaged members of a community.

- Work actively to enhance the leadership capacity of community members, leaders, and groups within the community.

- Be open to using the full range of action strategies to work toward the long term sustainability and well being of the community.

We view community development as a profession that integrates knowledge from many disciplines with theory, research, teaching, and practice as important and interdependent functions that are vital in the public and private sectors. We believe the Society must be proactive by providing leadership to professionals and citizens across the spectrum of community development. In so doing, we believe the Society must be open and responsive to the needs of its members through provisions and services which enhance professional development.